ON GUARD!

Photo: Wilson Gould Studios

LT-COL. A. J. H. SLOGGETT, D.S.O.
Commanding Officer, 10th (Torbay) Battalion, 1941–1945, and Rex

ON GUARD!

A History of the
10th (Torbay) Battalion
Devonshire Home Guard

Edited by

G. H. LIDSTONE

Published by the Battalion Publication Committee

C. H. FURSDON, E.D.
VICTOR H. GOULD
H. BERKELEY HOLLYER, M.M.
P. T. READ, M.B.E., M.M.

The Naval & Military Press Ltd

Published by

The Naval & Military Press Ltd
Unit 10 Ridgewood Industrial Park,
Uckfield, East Sussex,
TN22 5QE England

Tel: +44 (0) 1825 749494
Fax: +44 (0) 1825 765701

www.naval-military-press.com
www.nmarchive.com

In reprinting in facsimile from the original, any imperfections are inevitably reproduced and the quality may fall short of modern type and cartographic standards.

Dedicated to ....

the Spirit of Loyalty and Service which, born of travail and adversity, made of civilian soldiers a united and integral part of our country's defence ; a Spirit of Comradeship and Sacrifice which strengthened our faith and warmed our hearts and has a place, if we will but employ it, in the happier days of Peace

FOREWORD

by the Rt. Hon. Sir James Grigg

K.C.B., K.C.S.I., Secretary of State for War, 1942—45

THE NATION owes an incalculable debt to the self-sacrifice and devotion of those men who have given, willingly and cheerfully, so many hours of their leisure to service in the Home Guard.

Without their help the armies—or at any rate some of them—which are now liberating one country after another from the Germans, could not have left this country.

The Home Guard have, it is true, never been called upon to engage the enemy—much to the disappointment of its members, I may say, but all the same their presence in Great Britain has ensured the safety of the base from which the expeditionary forces have been launched and are being maintained.

Moreover, the Home Guard have made a very effective contribution to the defence of our homes against attacks by aircraft and flying bombs.

As I am myself a Devonian I am naturally inclined to think that the County which produced (among others) John Duke of Marlborough, Drake, Raleigh, Gilbert, Hawkins, Charles Kingsley, John Gay, and Sir Joshua Reynolds, must have produced some of the best Home Guard Battalions in the country, and that consequently this record of the activities of the 10th Devon Battalion should make good reading.

1945

Contents

Chapter		Page
	Foreword	5
	Preface	7
1	History Repeated	9
2	The Early Days	13
3	Growing Pains	19
4	Reaching Maturity	27
5	Inland Defence	33
6	Memorable Nights	37
7	Guarding the Coast	45
8	The Palace Raid	55
9	Paignton L.D.V.	59
10	Reorganisation	69
11	Nocturne in F	73
12	Brixham's Zeal	81
13	H.Gs. Destroy F.W.190	87
14	Gun Site Tragedy	103
	Past Members	107
	Present Members (December, 1944)	125

PREFACE

UNLIKE the remainder of this book, which will, I hope, be of interest to a wider readership than the Home Guard, this preface is directed to members of the 10th Battalion, some of whom have exercised commendable patience, and others who have been audibly impatient in what has admittedly been a long time to wait for this publication.

Of the contents of this book I make no apology. The information was provided either by the companies concerned or by people who should know the answers, and although as a history it cannot, of course, be regarded as complete, it is given as extensively as the paper supply permits and fairly summarises the Battalion's activities.

For the choice of material, putting some in and taking some out, I naturally accept full responsibility. It was not always easy to decide what was of the greatest interest and it is a matter of real regret that many people will be disappointed that the incidents they so kindly recounted have not found a place. So much for the contents—except to thank those who helped me circumvent the many obstacles that Fate (and just a few unco-operative souls) had strewn along the editorial path. It is not my intention to enumerate those of whose efforts acknowledgment would normally be made. But as a palliative to my own conscience I must mention the two people whom I badgered most—Lt.-Col. P. L. Coleridge, whose cartoons and manuscript (both received when enthusiasm was at a pretty low ebb) form the nuclei of the production, and Mr. Victor Gould, who undertook to look after the photographic side and performed marvels with the most unpromising negatives. To both of them, to the Publication Committee which has given solid support throughout, and to all who came to the rescue at one time or another—a sincere " Thank you."

The delay in publishing the book has been occasioned by the paper shortage. The Publication Committee determined—rightly, in my view—that the Battalion was worthy of something better than a pamphlet which would not permit of illustrations, and decided that a book should be prepared for the press and then await the lifting of restrictions. That moment has arrived—and this is the product. I hope you will like it, though I believe its value will be more apparent in years to come when the names of our old compatriots in Home Guard ranks begin to grow hazy and dim. Memories are notoriously short, and in the preparation of this book the ease with which one forgets the good and the bad has been very noticeable. That is why it has been so difficult to recapture the spirit of the Home Guard, which was the very essence of our undertaking. They were often irksome days, those days of the Volunteer Force, though not without their compensating features, but now it is over we can see the brighter side of incidents that caused heart-burning at the time and can accept with a smile the witticism of a newspaper correspondent who said an appropriate medal ribbon for the Home Guard would be a piece of red tape browned-off at both ends !

Red tape—yes. If we had much more we would have perished of strangulation, but there was no question of being browned-off either at the beginning or the end.

We simply had a streak of cussedness and a penchant for being awkward. We still have it—as you will hear if you gate-crash a Home Guard reunion. Somewhere you will hear him grousing as he groused in 1940—of the quality of his officers, the inexperience of N.C.Os., the absurdity of the strong points, the unreasonable lack of transport, the inconvenience of duty hours, the unfairness of the rota, the smallness of the rations—and the futility of the whole affair.

His name ? Well, no name, no pack drill, but you will recognise him in any section as the old-and-faithful, the reliable so-and-so, the hard diamond who never let you down—the corner stone of the L.D.V. and, in the fullness of time, the main pillar of the Home Guard.

The Editor.

August, 1946

CHAPTER 1

Invasion, as a possibility, was not new to Torbay. Men grabbed hay forks and cudgels to defend their homes 100 years ago.

With the Call for Local Defence,

HISTORY REPEATED

THE most obvious place at which to begin this narrative would appear to be the beginning. Not an original declaration, the reader may decide, but this book may take many unexpected twists and turns, so, defying precedent and custom, let us go back a century or more before the urgent appeal broadcast by the Rt. Hon. Anthony Eden, the then Secretary of State for War—back to the days of Napoleon, the Corsican, who, like his counterpart of the Twentieth Century, lived only for the sweets of conquest.

They were anxious days, for Torbay was never free from the threat of invasion, rumours were rife and even at their work men kept one eye towards the Channel. There was a voluntary mobilisation. Toothless mariners who had left the Deep Waters for the tranquility of the peaceful though industrious port of Brixham ; fishermen from the tiny, unknown and unfashionable village that was later to become Torquay ; traders from the prosperous little town of Paignton and hardy sons of the soil from the fertile lands that skirt the Bay trod paths which, in another war, and another age, their successors wearing L.D.V. armlets were destined to follow.

Napoleon and Hitler had one great thing in common. Both knew that while Britain lived no victory could be complete ; both realised that to those who dwell in this " sceptred isle " there has for ever been an innate sympathy for the underdog. Both determined to suppress the spirit of this race. Both, therefore, built a fleet of flat-bottomed barges. And both, for much the same reason, " missed the boat."

It might, of course, have been another story, for in the early 1800's the most that Torbay, which offered many landing places for these small craft, could do was to fortify Berry Head, but it was clear that unless reinforcements could answer the call of the warning in time, Torbay, at least, would pass to the French.

That they would first have had to run the gauntlet of old fowling pieces, flint-locks and hay forks there can be no doubt, for Torbay was prepared to fight. Even evacuation was arranged, and those whose fighting days were over were to travel with the women and children to the hinterland of Dartmoor. Transport was by farm carts !

History records that Napoleon did reach Torbay on July 24th, 1815—but on board His Majesty's man-o'war *Belerophon*, from which, having first come on deck to admire the beauties of the Bay, he was transferred off Berry Head to the *Northumberland*—and so to St. Helena.

The fate of Hitler is not quite so clear, but had the Navy produced him as they did Napoleon, Home Guardsmen of the 10th Battalion would not have been at a loss for suggestions. Whatever the unhappy destination to which they would have consigned him, his presence in Torbay would have afforded the part-time warriors of 1940-45 the same grim pleasure that their predecessors derived on that summer morning over a century ago.

Let us admit that Home Guard personnel are as relieved as those stout-hearted worthies of the past that the threat of invasion has gone. We are glad—for we may herein be frank—that after four and a half years of incessant training and constant strain the authorities were able to disband the Force.

It was a long road and a hard one for those of our number who did the work of three by day and carried out the duties of uniformed, disciplined soldiers by night. But the end did arrive and, despite the view of columnists who appeared to think the Home Guard so popular that we would never want our " ticket," the day of the " Stand Down " will be a memorably happy one to men with homes and gardens and old enthusiasms to recapture. It would be hypocrisy to pretend otherwise.

SGT. F. WISEMAN (F2. Platoon) typifies the Local Defence Volunteers of the pre-denim era of 1940

The Local Defence Volunteer Force was formed for a specific purpose. Even the most optimistic agreed that in the days of Dunkirk the most we could do was to delay the enemy, to give the Regulars, hastily reforming after the withdrawal from Belgium, valuable breathing space. Had the Hun arrived the L.D.Vs. would have gone into battle with nothing but Faith in the Right, broomsticks, shotguns and a calculated determination to obtain the scalp of at least one German parachutist. The lack of firepower was compensated—as far as it could be—by British grit, but wars are not won by courage alone and we know that, contrary to the advice of Officialdom, a tough young Nazi, armed to the teeth, descending from the blue with a sub-machine gun in one hand and a grenade in the other is not the easiest prey.

We were told that a cudgel was our finest weapon ; that a parachutist would always be at a disadvantage at the moment of landing. How to place ourselves at the precise spot at the exact time and bearing the recommended weapon (for even walking sticks were difficult to obtain !) was a major problem.

But the main job was one of observation. So much water has flowed beneath the bridge since May 12th, 1940, and so many changes taken place in the duties of the Force, to say nothing of the changes in military strategy, all of which we were expected to master in our stride, that it is not easy to recapture the spirit of the first patrols. We accepted the instructions of the butcher, baker or candlestick maker—good fellows all—never questioning their authority and not knowing who commanded us or what powers were vested in us. One thing, however, was made clear. Our duty was to observe and, in the event of an enemy landing (Rotterdam having proved a practice ground for the paratroop technique it was anticipated that the Germans' attack would be air-borne rather than sea-borne) report to the police by telephone or runner—and then continue to observe. Not until the first issue of weapons was it seriously suggested that we might prove a match for the enemy, and even to the last day of our effective service the emphasis was always on the words " Observe—Report."

But to return to the " good old days " of the Volunteers, as a synopsis of what other writers will describe throughout this book, take your minds back to the first week.

Men in all walks of life and all ages, grouped in threes and fours under a patrol leader (chosen, in some cases with justification perhaps, because he was either on the telephone or owned a car and was therefore able to contact his " chosen few ") were told the limits of their patrol, the hours of darkness to be covered and the nights for which they were responsible, and then left to it to hammer out the details for themselves.

This was Democracy at work. Good-natured chaffing sometimes led to bickering and honest-to-goodness grousing ; men felt free to say what they pleased and did not lose the opportunity—but from it all was fashioned a force which, dependent upon loyalty alone, really worked.

The eagerness with which men volunteered for the most unpopular " watches " and obeyed unquestioningly at short notice instructions reaching them on back of enve

Battalion Mascot JOHN ATKINS unofficially on the strength of A1. Platoon whose parades he attended with unfailing regularity

lopes, odd pieces of paper or quite casually by someone who had "heard it said," was an inspiration, and in days when one knew not what to believe, it restored confidence in their generation and bared for the world to see—if it cared—the depth of their desire to serve.

Early musketry instruction was lapped up. Night after night men in Torquay, Paignton and Brixham herded into small, smoke-laden rooms to re-learn what many had learned in World War I. There were 12-bore sporting guns, an occasional Ross, an S.M.L.E. was issued and withdrawn in the same week, and then came what every man had awaited in a fervour—his own rifle, packed in grease, from the U.S.A.

The P17 had arrived. The B.A.R. followed. Then came the Browning, Vickers and Lewis machine guns, the Thompson sub-machine gun, the Spigot Mortar, the Smith gun, McNaughten tubes, the Sten carbine, grenades, anti-tank mines and all the paraphernalia of a well-equipped modern army, to which the Home Guard had graduated through stages of civvies, brassards and denims.

Officers, N.C.Os. and men of the 10th (Torbay) Bn. were well exercised and there were times, be it noted, when they were more than a match for their Regular opponents, but the occasion for fighting the real enemy on the beaches and in the fields never came.

To say we regretted the absence of the Hun would be a poor acknowledgment of the bravery of the gallant youngsters who first drew enemy blood, and of the men and women of all three services who gave their lives to prevent the invasion that Home Guards trained to resist.

But, being human, there were times when, with sorrows of our own, we thought longingly of targets other than those so painstakingly prepared by Mr. Field-Fisher and his staff. That was surely understandable.

They drilled with anything that came to hand—broomsticks, if necessary—for the days (and nights) of 1940 belonged to the enthusiasts and the doughty.

CHAPTER 2

Thanks to Lieut.-Col. P. L. Coleridge's vivid memory we here record something at least of the hopes, illusions and successes of 1940.

Problems and personalities of

THE EARLY DAYS

TO describe the formation of what later became the 10th Bn. (Torbay) Home Guard, I am taking you back to May 14th, 1940, when Mr. Anthony Eden, the Secretary of State for War, broadcast an appeal for Volunteers as anti-Parachutists.

There was an immediate response in the three Torbay towns and by May 22nd it was possible to convene a meeting at Torquay Police Station for the purpose of forming a company of the Local Defence Volunteers, stationed as follows :

Platoons I and 2 ...	Torquay
Platoon 3 ...	Paignton
Platoon 4 ...	Brixham (with Churston, Galmpton and Kingswear)

The company commander and company second-in-command had already been appointed—C.C., Lt.-Col. R. Despard Davies (Indian Army, Retired), Paignton ; second-in-command, Major W. F. Ball, T.D. (Devon Regiment—T.), Torquay.

There was an absolute dearth of maps, but the company area was based on a Police Divisional Map loaned for the occasion, and makeshift copies were hurriedly traced.

It was decided that Torquay should be divided into :

RURAL AREA ...	No. I Platoon
COASTAL AREA ...	No. 2 Platoon

Lt.-Col. P. L. Coleridge (Indian Army, Retired) was invited to command No. I Platoon, assisted by Captain T. A. Codner (late Royal Artillery) and Captain M. G. Hart (late Tank Corps) ; and Major E. W. K. Bennett became the first O.C. of No. 2 Platoon.

A list of possible section leaders (for Torquay only) was compiled and handed to the Police with a request that they should be invited to attend for interview on the morrow at the Police Station, but there was extreme difficulty in getting anyone to take on the duties of section leader. " And they with one consent began to make excuse."

Results were most disheartening. Many reasons may be

LT.-COL. R. DESPARD DAVIES
First C.O. of the Torbay Battalion—
'an early labourer in the vineyard'

advanced, among them a fear of being out of pocket over stationery, telephone, postages and petrol; a very real (if not widespread) doubt as to the intentions of the Government as to possible " variation of conditions of service," once the men were enrolled; and the attitude of a certain section of the Press. Some " boosting " had already gone on, the keynote of which was absolute equality ! " No Officers—no N.C.Os." " If you have a grievance you can quit after giving 14 days' notice."

While on the one hand an officer holding the highest Army rank was addressing meetings and saying the L.D.V. was to constitute a part of the Forces of the Crown, certain petty ink-slinging scribblers were doing their utmost to stigmatize the nascent corps as a vile rabble. Some persons *had* to accept responsibility; someone *had* to do the spade work, someone *had* to receive and distribute arms, equipment, and clothing; someone, with past military experience, *had* to supervise training, musketry, &c., and yet, *in time of war*, these irresponsible individuals were out to decry all idea of leadership of any kind, and the bedrock of discipline, with side-long excursions into a web of balderdash connected with " blimpery," " old school tie," " obese majors," and other cheap sneers at ex-officers varying in degree of virulence with their rank. Thus, at the very commencement, the organisation of the L.D.V. had a set-back.

In the meantime the company commander (Lt. Col. Despard Davies) had contacted a former Staff Sergeant Major, Mr. F. A. Larkworthy, and they succeeded in " capturing " the Old Town Hall at Torquay, which had been the H.Q. of a Home Defence Company and was about to be vacated.

The Torbay Company L.D.V. now had its H.Q. *and* a Sergeant Major !

The Company H.Q. opened on May 24th, but in view of the distance the Paignton and Brixham platoons " ran their own show," which was a mercy ! A scene of extraordinary confusion prevailed. There was little furniture, little stationery (and what there was was purchased by the Commanding Officer at his own expense), and no transport except a few private cars. Nevertheless, enrolling commenced, and interruptions—already innumerable—increased with the establishment of the telephone. Men who had come to be enrolled were kept standing about indefinitely, while the hapless enrollers ran out of forms and bawled for more !

By May 25th some hitherto unknown " Superior Authorities " had taken the field and a vague attempt was made by someone to lay down an " establishment "—a section strength of 25 ! ! This was soon cancelled.

A more military aspect of affairs was imparted by the arrival from "somewhere in Devon" of sixteen .303 1914 pattern rifles and 160 rounds of S.A.A., which the C.O. ordered to be distributed at the rate of four rifles and 40 rounds per platoon.

It may here be stated that most of these rifles were dirty, although greasy and packed in strong cartons. One, however, which was handed to No. 1 Platoon, was apparently gifted with second sight and arrived naked, but *fully loaded*, one round in the chamber and four in the magazine ! !

On May 27th, 1940, the C.O. made his official debut at his new H.Q. and Col. Coleridge relieved Maj. Ball as second-in-command and handed over No. 1 Platoon to Captain Hart.

LT.-COL. P. COLERIDGE, O.B.E.

O.C. the original No. 1 Platoon and then second-in-command of the Torbay Battalion

May 28th.—The C.O. was summoned to Exeter to "report progress" and receive instructions and returned with dire news from the War Front—and dire news for the L.D.V. ! The state of its armament was ignored, and an individual was alleged to have waxed fanatical. Volunteers were to become "savages." If no rifles were available "there were sticks, and stones, bludgeons, pitchforks, pickaxes and shovels !" At the same time a lurid picture of enemy parachutists was painted—young men, highly trained, each bearing two or more sub-machine guns and floating earthwards with an easily detachable bomb tied to each foot ready for instant release on any lurking L.D.V. ' dervish ' !

So ended the first week of the L.D.V's existence in Torquay.

Space obviously forbids a further day by day narrative. The platoon commanders duly met at H.Q. and the office began to function. Captain E. J. S. Gough, M.M., was enrolled and began to assist the Sergeant-Major in enrolling men. A.F. 3066 began to appear properly printed, as did some official brassards purveyed by the D.T.A. But there was no Quartermaster's department as yet. Zone H.Q. began to blossom at Chudleigh and vied with the D.T.A. in an increasing bombardment of A.C's and other 1's, and also other literature. The local Special Constabulary and Coastguard began to scent a military aroma about the, as yet virtually unarmed, L.D.V., and demanded a "guard" for a petrol dump and harbour piquets. These demands, it is needless to say, were bluntly turned down.

There were four acute problems facing H.Q. These should be noted.

(1) *Discipline and Conditions of Service.*

Everyone was on the same footing and, while signing a form pledging submission to Military Law, enjoyed the privilege of being permitted to terminate his agreement to serve, with 14 days' notice. There was no provision for Commissions for the "officers" or legal status for N.C.Os. It may here be pointed out that a Commission is a Royal Warrant *ordering* in the name of the Sovereign unquestioning *obedience* to all legal orders issued by the holder of such Commission, while N.C.Os are catered for in the Manual of Military Law and King's Regulations, and have certain authority under such.

Other difficulties arose, such as responsibility for the care and custody of Government property of a very costly nature, and the custody and proper disbursement of Government cash.

Again, as regards the performance of military duties, the vast majority of L.D.Vs were men in employment or running their own businesses ; they were only available for routine duty when such business closed for the day. The day duties demanded by the authorities could only, therefore, be performed by " whole-timers," gentlemen of leisure (!), unemployed, and pensioners. The strength available for day duties was therefore very small and involved spells of duty of 6—8 hours. So long as this was confined to O.P. work it was not impossible, but when the duties of a sentry were casually imposed, complications arose. But these difficulties and hardships were never visualised and everything was to be overcome, and set aside, by a sense of broad-minded willingness and fervid patriotism.

(2) *Armament and Equipment.*

However much the " Mahdi " of Exeter might rant on "savage instincts," the men were naturally very keen to be armed and equipped as soldiers (more or less). Delay was absolutely unavoidable in view of the military situation, but many waxed impatient. An appeal by the Government for shot guns met a fair response, but the supply of ammunition was meagre, and in any case the shot guns proved unpopular.

(3) *Clothing.*

Next to arms and equipment, the men wanted some sort of uniform. They had been promised " suits, denim," but the issue hung fire and even brassards were slow in putting in an appearance.

" Brewing up "—one of the more heartening sights during moorland exercises.

Even pigeons did their duty! "Attached" to Signals they co-operated in exercises and demonstrated their zeal at the Birthday Parade.

Home-made ones of various colours were at first donned, until Captain H. R. G. Moore, R.N., retired, obtained some fawn-coloured cloth from which brassards were manufactured by a Ladies' Working Party, the lettering being of white tape. However, the D.T.A. began to send in brassards in ever-increasing numbers, though, like the rifles, our first issue of "suits, denim," was but a "token one."

There were unexpected "snags" in the fitting of suits, and the experiment was first carried out privily (!) at H.Q. They were duly packed in sizes, and the contractors were obsessed with the idea that a man 40in. round the perimeter *must be* 6ft. 3in. tall. Mr. Larkworthy first underwent the ordeal and when he found a pair of trousers which would duly meet, he inevitably discovered his feet encased in a large surplus, or else the waistband was around his ears. It was clear that some "fitting under local arrangements" would be necessary in most cases, and who was to pay the piper? After some correspondence the D.T.A. agreed that this was a fair charge against them, and arrangements were made with local tradesmen whose bills for alterations after due "vetting" were passed for payment.

By now a Q.M. stores was established at H.Q. and Captain Laing became Quartermaster assisted by Mr. C. Wilson, and clothing and equipment began to arrive in ever-increasing quantities.

(4) *Training*.

Last, but by no means least, Mr. C. H. Field-Fisher was made Musketry Instructor, got together sundry assistants and commenced a series of evening classes which were remarkably well attended.

Then the original sixteen .303 rifles were withdrawn, and replaced by Ross "straight pull" rifles. These were mistrusted (possibly the straight pull action was the cause) and produced another problem for H.Q.

MAJOR W. F. BALL, T.D.
Second-in-command, later succeeded by Lt.-Col. P. L. Coleridge, and later again second-in-command to Lt.-Col. Sloggett

Certain L.D.V.s., finding night duty monotonous, insisted on removing the bolts from their Ross rifles and found they could not put them back! This was rather tricky, needing deft manipulation of the bolt head, and, finding the bolt stubborn, they used force. Result: damage to rifle, and the need of an armourer's shop!!

Fortunately the Torquay L.D.V. possessed a very experienced armourer in Mr. J. A. Scudamore, who quickly established himself in the Clock Tower at H.Q. Tools were more than scarce, but he devised his own to a very large extent and had them made locally.

Notwithstanding their disappointment at the delay in arming and uniforming them, the men got down to drill, and a certain amount of spade work at the various posts. As an illustration of the good spirit prevailing, the following episode may be cited: It had been decided to place some coast defence guns on Corbyn's Head. On the evening of June 25th, 1940, the Naval officer i/c. Port Defences rang H.Q. The guns had arrived, but no gunners. Could the L.D.V. do anything in the way of a guard?

A musketry lecture was being held at the time, and volunteers were called for. More than twice the number of men needed volunteered at once.

The scene at the mounting of the guard was not pleasant. Civilian labour had been employed and, the hour of 5 p.m. having struck, the labourers had cleared off. Railings lay strewn around. One gun had been mounted, and draped in odd tarpaulins, while the concrete was setting, but the other lay on a small trolley rather on its side, but pointing grimly at—*The Grand Hotel.*

A bored, and seemingly slightly intoxicated workman lounged at the gate of the 'enclosure,' which had ceased to be such, and gave one to understand that he was only waiting for the " milling-tary " before he " 'opped it " ! ! !

He lost no time in doing so.

MR. C. H. FIELD-FISHER
Musketry Officer from whom L.D.Vs received their first weapon training

" The Arabs taught me that no man could be their leader except he ate the ranks' food, wore their clothes, lived level with them and yet appeared better in himself."

T. E. Lawrence
Seven Pillars of Wisdom.

CHAPTER 3

The youngster was growing in stature and experience, but instruction from "outside mentors" did not make for peace of mind!

With development came the

GROWING PAINS

THE Torbay L.D.V. Company now had some "attached platoons" of a specialised nature, organised for defence of Utility Undertakings, &c.

These were : (1) Gas Company ; (2) Post Office ; (3) Electricity Dept. ; (4) G.W.R. ; (5) Devon General Omnibus Co.

To these were added a platoon recruited from the staff of the Prudential Assurance Company, who had evacuated to Torquay, and the whole six were dubbed H.Q. Platoons, to be sponsored by the second-in-command. The Prudential, under Mr. A. Coombs, furnished the night telephonists at Company H.Q.

The days of the L.D.V. Company were now numbered, and, with ever-increasing expansion, it passed by not very easy stages into a battalion of five Companies.

Torquay H.Q. Coy. O.C. Lt.Col. P. L. Coleridge, O.B.E.
   ,, A. Coy.   ,, Captain T. A. Codner.
   ,, B. Coy.   ,, Captain H. R. G. Moore, C.B.E.
Paignton C. Coy.   ,, Major E. H. Woosley, O.B.E.
   ,, D. Coy.   ,, Captain Hay Matthey (who resigned in favour of Lt-Col. W. L. Parsons).

The office work at Battalion H.Q. at this time was enormous, and there was a shortage of clerical workers, as the companies, now being more or less self-contained units, were naturally loath to part with capable men. A most valuable "recruit" appeared in the person of Lt.-Col. K. E. Cooper, M.C. (Indian Army, Retired) and Col. Davies placed him in charge of "Operations Sections."

H.Q. looked imposing on paper !

O.C. Battalion ... ... Lt.-Col. R. Despard Davies.
Second-in-command and
  O.C. H.Q. Coy. ... ... Lt.-Col. P. L. Coleridge, O.B.E.
Operations ... ... Lt.-Col. K. E. Cooper, M.C.
Quartermaster ... ... Captain Laing.
Office Supervisor ... ... S.Sgt.-Maj. F. A. Larkworthy.
Records ... ... Captain E. J. Gough, M.M.

CAPT. J. ROBYNS
The Battalion's first Home Guard Adjutant

To these were added :
Intelligence ... ... Major W. F. Ball, T.D.
Liaison Officer ... Capt. F. J. March.
    and again, later :
Adjutant ... ... Capt. J. Robyns.
But there were no typists, and no typewriters !

By July the picture had greatly changed. The new battalion had a strength of close on 2000 ; 300 American .303 rifles were received with a fair supply of ammunition and a cascade of denims ; the Home Guard was formed, and the L.D.V. vanished.

Work in the Home Guard might be grouped under two headings :
(A.) Training so as to be fit to play its part in repelling a possible enemy invasion.
(B.) Administration.

Despite having to be carried on in the evenings, on half holidays *and* Sundays " A " was " romantic " on the whole, and much played up to by the military authorities. " B " was the daily round, operated by a comparatively small number, *unromantic*, and badly left out in the cold by the military authorities. Several inspections were carried out by high ranking officers, but these were entirely confined to work in the field and never once did senior officers of " Q " branch visit us in the office or aid us in tackling difficult administrative problems. Evasion was the key-note of this side of the picture, and it was virtually impossible to contact any " competent financial authority " among the military.

Reverting to " A," apart from elementary drill, " Defence " was the mainspring of training ; Road Blocks and Defended Areas loomed large and these were extended to " Beach Defences."

Finally came Musketry, relegated to the last place owing to the acute shortage of practice ammunition.

Road Blocks, constructed by civilian labour and sited by the R.E., began to sprout, but as they were to be (1) elaborated by the H.G. (that is to say *made the centres* of defended areas) and (2) manned by the H.G. at *short notice*, it was imperative they should be within easy reach of their prospective H.G. garrisons.

This was not always considered, and Col. Cooper spent many an hour wrestling with this problem. The worst defended area conundrum was at a place in " D " Company Area, called Hill Head. As certain officers were of opinion that to man a position around Hill Head would require a Brigade there was some " despondency " if not alarm in " D " Company, which was the weakest in numbers in the battalion !

But minor Defended Areas and Beach Defences were the peculiar " pigeon " of " B " Company. Captain Moore was a firm believer in sand and sand-bags. He indented for tons of the former and thousands of the latter. He got *some*, but as all his platoon wanted to " do their bit," and " B " Company seemed short of ex-Sappers, the sand bags were scattered. Here and there an admirable work was planted, but, as a set-off, many others, sown promiscuously over the area, " dissolved " in bad weather. But *nil desperandum* was the motto of " B " Company. More evening working parties paraded. A few new sand-bags were introduced—the badly-behaved ones were re-filled, and soundly spanked with shovels—and their last stage was sometimes worse than their first !

CAPT. F. J. MARCH
Former Adjutant/Quartermaster ; then Quartermaster. Transferred in 1943 to the 8th Somerset Battn.

Things went from bad to worse when " A " Company caught the sand-bag fever. A young " Malakoff " appeared at Cockington and sundry hedgerows near Gallows Gate suffered a sand-bag visitation. On the other hand a road block near Watcombe, although imperfect, was commended officially. " C " Company fared much better, and did some wonderfully good work on Paignton sea front and elsewhere in their area.

On July 19th the Military Liaison Officer and Zone Commander came to inspect road blocks, but as they limited it to an afternoon they did not get very far.

Other military officers began to carry out inspections and shortly " Stop Lines " and " Battle Positions " began to oust the road blocks (or most of them). In the midst of this, circumstances compelled Col. Cooper to reside elsewhere, and he left Torquay to the very real regret of everyone at Battalion H.Q. He was relieved in August, 1940, by Lt.-Col. A. J. H. Sloggett, D.S.O., late Rifle Brigade, who resided in Paignton.

Meanwhile, the situation of the battalion as regards its operational role became involved. It was rather suggestive of the Tuscan Army in Macaulay's " Lays of Ancient Rome," when it met with a " sharp reverse " at the hands of " brave Horatius " and his two staunch companions.

> But those behind cried " Forward ! "
> And those before cried " Back ! "

It was then that a certain officer on his way to taking up a Staff appointment " up country " appeared on the scene and apparently in consultation with the O.C. Troops in the neighbourhood traced a line on a map of Torquay and proceeded to reconnoitre it, accompanied on the first day by Lt.-Col. Sloggett and other representatives of Battalion H.Q. and on the second by the C.O. (Lt.-Col. Despard Davies) in person. This " line " evidently favoured those who cried " Back ! "

Barton, a great portion of Chelston, the old O.Ps, and various road blocks, including the " prize " one at Watcombe, were to be

Little credit, little praise, but good comrades. Battalion D.Rs., whose job was not always the sinecure the gun teams would have us believe!

abandoned. Harsh treatment was also meted out to " B " Company's " cock shies." The whole scheme was to be based on in-fighting, to say nothing of street fighting ; the aid of the Sappers was to be invoked, and the H.G. was to do most of the wiring—if not all. Paignton and Brixham were to link up, but whether this officer actually went over the ground in those areas also, the present writer cannot say. This officer was diffident in expressing a positive estimate of the *strength* required to man his " line," but when pressed he somewhat tardily issued an estimate which worked out considerably in excess of the rifle strength then in existence !

But " The Delamaine Line " abode on paper as a sort of bogey to haunt the C.O. and, although the Sappers were slow in coming, more rifles, some light automatics and machine guns of American origin arrived.

A rather evil phrase also put in an appearance, which was apparently much liked at Zone H.Q. This was " When the Balloon goes up," but mere reading the words in black and white does not do it justice. It had to be uttered in a sepulchral tone, if not *sotto voce*, accompanied by a rather furtive glance ! ! If committed to paper it had to be labelled **" Secret."**

However, with much consideration of the ascent of a balloon, it dawned on the authorities that a certain amount of range practice with Service ammunition was desirable. Some miniature rifles, and a goodly supply of ammunition existed and a considerable amount of miniature rifle shooting had been carried out, " B " Company having " captured," and their Cpl. Markham having put into fine working order, the covered .22 range at Walls Hill.

But no amount of miniature shooting can take the place of the " real thing." Mr. Field-Fisher and his " staff " got together by hook and by crook material for targets, and a number of men were exercised in "grouping."

The fame of the range having been noised abroad, a Regular unit borrowed it, and having shot the targets to pieces, went on its way, without one word of gratitude, and no offer to pay for the damage. This was hardly a courteous act, and involved some expenditure of cash, labour and bad language by the H.G.! The range was extended to 300 yards with some later aid by the military, who placed a firing point on the roof of a public convenience (ladies' section) which in peacetime had been allowed to trespass on the then disused range. Happily, the said convenience had already been closed!

Practice, if inclined to be spasmodic, and the trying out of automatic weapons, proceeded with increasing success, and the labours of Mr. Field-Fisher and his staff in these early days deserve to be set on record. They indeed worked very hard under not always encouraging conditions.

The administrative side of the picture was one of almost unbroken gloom. . . . A perfect spate of correspondence descended on Battalion H.Q. and there was no trained clerical staff to cope with it. Everything had to be created. Moreover, the nature of the correspondence was peculiar. Possibly to save stationery, an abominable system of "omnibus" letters and memos was brought into use. Or possibly it was a strategic move to ensure these documents being read carefully. All sorts of subjects were compressed into a number of paragraphs on one sheet, training cheek by jowl with administrative details. Frequently these documents contained odd matters of a confidential or secret nature, but these were sandwiched into a lot of quite ordinary routine matter. This rendered

The "brains of the outfit." Personnel of the Intelligence Section photographed at Exeter aerodrome awaiting a reconnaissance flight.

any sensible system of filing impossible and protests, albeit couched in civil language, were politely ignored.

Some figures now may be of interest. For the first month after its inception the Battalion claims for subsistence allowance were round about £700, for the second month over £800 and for the third over £900. This caused some acrid correspondence, and the D.T.A. demanded "vouchers in support," "duty sheets," &c., but omitted to mention they had supplied any or *authorised* the purchase of such. "C" Company had devised and purchased their own privately, and the H.Q. Company platoons did likewise: the other companies had little material to go on. What was the cause of the steady rise in the amount of the claims ? It was certainly *not* due to a steady increase in the strength of the battalion. It was due to a free translation of the motto *Carpe Diem* : The very term " period of continuous duty " was vague—*when* did a man come on duty ? When he left his home, or when he reported at his post or assembly point of his patrol ? Again, what was a reasonable time for him to take in transit ? Further, were men employed on clerical duties at Battalion or Company H.Q. to be eligible or not ? It is easy to say " No," their duties were *not* continuous, but on occasion they were asked to lend a hand in unloading stores, &c., and so missed their lunch ! Try as one might to convince the men that subsistence allowance was to compensate for outlay on purchasing some forms of " subsistence " while on duty, it was looked upon as a meagre kind of compensation for duty performed in lieu of regular pay.

Nor was ingenuity in preferring claims confined to the mere " rank and file." A few sub-unit " commanders " began to live in a perennial state of " duty "—for instance one claimed he had, while at his business, to be in a constant state of " stand to " for possible telephone calls from Battalion and Company H.Q.—while another apparently lived entirely without sleep ! !

It was now decided to do something towards conferring the invidious distinction of Ranks on the H.G. This took the form of a few chevrons of orthodox type, and also the issue, at first by something like a fathom, but later in shorter lengths, of *blue* tape accompanied by instructions and scale drawings, for shoulder badges for " officers." The completed articles were perfected by Mr. March and sewn on to pieces of stiffened cloth to slip over the shoulder straps on " suits, denim." These were profanely dubbed " winkels " at Battalion H.Q., " winkel " being German for chevron, and having nothing to do with edible sea-snails !

Mr. Larkworthy and Captain Gough were at this time almost wallowing in A.F. 3066s but they got through the work somehow, and it was a happy day when they deposited a bale of these with the D.T.A. An Adjutant's " section " had been established with Captain J. Robyns as Adjutant.

As the battalion continued to progress, " casualties " occurred. Mr. Larkworthy fell to the lure of the newly created Mobile Section, which was organised entirely apart, and did not come under Battalion H.Q. To those who knew him and his work at the very commencement of things this was a sad loss, and the H.Q. office was not the same without him. Then Captain Robyns joined the Royal Navy and was succeeded by Captain March as Adjutant.

Capt. Gough resigned at 65, and in June 1941 Lt.Col. Davies, who resigned his Command and left Torquay, was succeeded by Lt.Col. Sloggett. The battalion was now a going concern, although untrained except in elementary drill and musketry.

But much spade work had been done in face of great difficulties, and sundry set-backs, and some credit is due to the early labourers in the vineyard !

Clothes maketh the man (Proverb).
A Battalion H.Q. Mannequin Parade.

CHAPTER 4

This chapter is compiled from the diary of Lieut.-Col. A. J. H. Sloggett, D.S.O., who took over command in June, 1941.

By 1942 the Battalion was steadily

REACHING MATURITY

THE first six months of 1941 had been spent chiefly in constructing the " Delamaine Line " and wiring the perimeters, excellent work in this respect being done by " A " Company on the Petitor golf links and in Cockington Park. The " Delamaine Line," or the Torquay landward defences, stretched from Petitor across country to the high ground north of the Hollacombe Gas Works, and consisted of numerous posts to hold six to ten men and machine guns. As this, a distance of four and a half miles, had to be held by one company, it was demonstrated in various exercises, that despite the view of higher authorities, it was an absolutely impracticable scheme.

The Paignton landward defence was the railway line, in places not more than 100 yards from the seashore, and of that subject no more will be said, though it must be admitted that a good landward defence for Paignton appeared to be an impossibility.

" Simla " and Saltern Head were both made into quite good defended localities. Broadsands was the most vulnerable part on our seaward side, and here there were no defences as it was impossible to find enough men for them.

Brixham was a nightmare. Many a wet and wearisome day was spent there with various Generals and our Group Commander, everybody having a different idea, and sharp contention arose as to the line on which the staunch H.Gs. of Brixham were to do or die " when the balloon went up." Finally a form of perimeter defence was made, consisting again of " penny packets " and quite impossible to hold. The spectre of Hill Head was laid and decently interred under a small road block !

The second half of 1941 found the battalion taking part in various exercises. There was the Brigade Tactical Exercise in which the 145th Infantry Brigade gave battle to three battalions of Home Guard (Torbay, Totnes, and Dartmouth) and battalions of the 1st Bucks and 10th Buffs, the Civil Defence exercise in which the battalion took part. the Brigade inter-communication exercise for all

CAPT. C. H. FURSDON, E.D.
Appointed to the Battalion in June, 1942, from the 8th Holsworthy Bn. as Adjutant

signals personnel, and day operations by the Paignton Home Guard with the 8th Buffs against the military and Home Guard of Dartmouth.

★ ★ ★

The year 1942 will long be remembered by us all for it was in March of that year that the enemy apparently decided that Torbay was worthy of attention, bombed Torquay harbour and sank the blockship " Stag " on March 31st, again visiting Torquay on April 25th. It was in this latter raid that Pte. Crocker of the battalion was killed. During June and August the Hun paid us two more visits and made life most unpleasant for a while, dropping his bombs without apparent plan of action or decent discrimination.

It was also in this year that the " Delamaine Line " went into well deserved retirement. During April and May it was decided that the Line was far too scattered into " penny packets " and certain " defence centres of resistance " were formed in its stead.

A close co-operation between the Home Guard and the Civil Defence was being built up and the excellent lectures by Major-General George Lindsay, the Deputy Regional Commissioner, did much to bring this about.

On May 17th we held our Second Anniversary Parade in Torquay and Paignton. And what a day it was. All on parade became wet through as there was driving rain all the time. Brixham were more lucky for they did not hold their anniversary parade until a fortnight later.

We were benefiting greatly by the kindness shown to us by the 8th Buffs, and those forty odd officers and N.C.Os. of the battalion who attended the battle practice under live shelling and mortar and small arms fire at Smeardon Down, Dartmoor, on June 9th, had a most interesting time.

It was in June that our Adjutant, Captain C. H. Fursdon, E.D., arrived. He had been transferred from the 8th (Holsworthy) Battalion Devon Home Guard in North Devon, where for a year and three months he had been Adjutant-Quartermaster. Captain March became Captain for " A " and " Q " duties only. The work had become too much for one man.

On July 8th the battalion was honoured by a visit of inspection by Major-General D. I. Johnson, V.C., then the Inspector General of Training, Home Guard. During his time with us he witnessed a demonstration of battlecraft in the Wall's Hill Quarry. Not only did he express great satisfaction at what he had seen, but later Major-General Mitchelmore (G.O.C. 77th Division) after watching the companies on exercises congratulated the Colonel on having the happiest battalion of Home Guards in his command. July had been a month of bouquets !

We were indeed sorry when our good friends the 8th Buffs left us on being transferred into S.E. Command, in September. During July, August and September, on every Sunday, they had kindly allowed us to send battle sections of an N.C.O. and seven men to the Haytor area to be put over the course by Lieut. Gardiner, their Training Officer, which was much appreciated by all who took part in it.

In September we moved out of our battalion headquarters at the Old Town Hall, and it was high time, too. A building antediluvian, uncomfortable and unbearable as regards draughts. Any window being opened resulted in a howling gale raging through the building, and why we were not all down with severe colds for the most part of the year was a miracle.

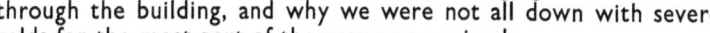

CAPT. W. H. FORSYTH
Late R.Q.M.S. 1st Bn. Liverpool Scottish, Bn. Quartermaster from April, 1943

Why we stayed so long is not known, but our Adjutant stirred us all up and was evidently solicitous about the health of his new Commanding Officer, or was it that he was prone to colds himself ? Anyhow, it was chiefly owing to his untiring efforts that we moved to our new battalion headquarters at Cambridge Lodge, Old Torwood Road, which had belonged to an old General of the Indian Army, and it was from his widow that we requisitioned it. Here was real comfort and a pleasant garden to look out upon, though shortly after our arrival the kitchen garden was captured by some bad little boys of the neighbourhood, who decamped with all the pears, much to the fury of our " gardener-connoisseur," the Adjutant.

Having seen many other battalion headquarters it can honestly be said that not one of them could compare with ours. Since then, as in the story book, we lived happily ever after.

★ ★ ★

One of the most memorable practices in which the battalion took part was the " Hawkins " Exercise, of which Brigadier Hewett (late Welch Regiment), G.O.C. 207 Infantry Brigade, was director. The exercise had been designed primarily to test out the workings of the Civil Defence Services and the Invasion Committee, and was to be a twenty-four hour show. The Home Guard had been asked to take part to create " atmosphere " and were told that they would not be disturbed.

And so with this sense of security Battalion H.Q. carried on through the night until roused, amid much coughing, by a sudden " Commando " raid and the arrival of a smoke grenade in the hall ! Everyone's dignity was distinctly ruffled at this breach of terms. This indeed was not cricket. Telephones rang, and buzzers buzzed until the director himself was contacted and we were allowed to continue unmolested.

MAJ. A. KNOLLYS, M.C. (decd.)
Former Records Officer and O.C.
'H' Company—"a most gallant gentleman"

But this had stirred our fighting blood, and after many appeals to be allowed to attack the enemy had been turned down permission was eventually given for a reprisal to be taken against his base at Torre Station if only with the idea of keeping all our opponents awake for the rest of the night.

In the meanwhile rumours filtered through to H.Q. that certain members of the Torquay Invasion Committee were trying to pluck up the courage to run the gauntlet of the several enemy patrols roaming about the town in order to gain a more secluded if not quite so comfortable a position in our combined alternative headquarters. Perhaps it was the promise of liberal bacon and eggs for breakfast that eventually settled their indecision.

And with the coming of dawn information was received that the enemy was preparing to move out of Torquay along the Babbacombe main road from the Strand and a counter attack was led against them by the Adjutant and C.S.M. Langley-Ellis (flourishing a Lewis gun) which, had it been staged a few minutes earlier, so it was ruled by the umpires, would have trapped their main body. As it was it succeeded in annihilating their rearguard to our great satisfaction.

Before the third anniversary arrived on May 16th, 1943, we had received a visit from The Viscount Bridgeman, Director General, Home Guard, during which he addressed a meeting of many officers at Battalion H.Q. We had also taken part in " Wings for Victory " parades.

During March the Paignton Home Guard, who were at the time organised as one double company, C1 and C2, under the command of Major Bentley and Major Hopkinson, was split into two complete and separate companies, designated " C " Company, under Major Wood, who was the administrative officer in the double company, and " F " Company, under Major Bentley. Major Hopkinson voluntarily took the lower rank of captain as he was unable to spare the time from his business, which took him away from Torbay at frequent intervals.

" C " Company took the southern portion of the town and " F " Company became responsible for the northern section, including Preston. This led to some discussion about the dividing boundary between the companies, for Major Bentley found his headquarters, which were at the Constitutional Club in Palace Avenue, on the wrong side of the road, and not being able to take the club with him put up a strong defence and succeeded in retaining his strategical position!

On April 26th Captain March left the battalion on being transferred to the 8th Somerset Bn. H.G., and on the following day his duties were taken over by Capt. W. H. Forsyth, late R.Q.M.S., 1st Battalion Liverpool Scottish.

On May 30th Torquay was raided by twenty-one Hun planes in daylight. The St. Marychurch church was destroyed during a children's service and about twenty-eight children were killed and twenty-three injured, and there were many other casualties in and around the Babbacombe area. Our Permanent Staff Instructor, C.S.M. Langley-Ellis, was away for the day on duty and on his return learnt that the flat in which he and his wife had been living had been completely destroyed. Mrs. Langley-Ellis was extremely lucky and it is a miracle how she escaped with minor injuries, for the part of the building which she was in was completely flattened.

C.S.M. G. A. LANGLEY-ELLIS
Popular P.S.I. Left in December, 1943, for the 24th (Hartland) Bn. as Captain and Adjutant

A number of Home Guards, chiefly from A1. Platoon, did splendid work and received strong commendations from the Civil Defence Authorities.

In early July the Commanding Officer started the idea of Sundays on Dartmoor, and we went there nearly every Sunday until mid-October. Schemes and field firing on Rippon Tor were generally attended by 200 to 250 men and all ranks enjoyed it.

On December 18th we bade farewell to our very popular P.S.I., C.S.M. Langley-Ellis, who was promoted to A/Captain and appointed Adjutant to the 24th (Hartland) Battalion Devon Home Guard.

And now for 1944. On January 18th the battalion suffered a great loss. Major Knollys, M.C., our Records Officer and O.C. " H " Company, died. A most gallant gentleman and very popular with us all. He lost a leg at Loos in 1917 while serving with the Grenadier Guards. His funeral on the 22nd at Shiphay Church was attended by 40 officers and 100 other ranks.

And then came the Battalion Manning Exercise on March 26th, a test of our dispositions and communications, the inspection being carried out by Brigadier Wyatt, M.C., T.D., Commanding Devon Sub-District, who sent inspecting officers to each locality armed with an imposing questionnaire to probe our weak spots. Proud we were later when we received their reports which, on the whole, were most satisfactory.

Enemy planes paid us a visit on May 29th, and though the German official communique later stated that the harbour installations at Torquay had been bombed, in fact he had succeeded in scattering bombs in Torquay, Chelston, Cockington and Marldon in a rather indiscriminate manner. Then, of course, came " D " Day.

Every chapter has an ending. To all of us it had been a happy and interesting time, not without its discomfort and its humorous incidents. The Home Guard movement, one of the finest our nation has ever had, had knit us together into one team, a band of brothers, and it was no doubt a great factor in the winning of the war.

Battalion Honoured

Captain P. T. Read, M.M., received the M.B.E. (Military Division) in 1944 " in recognition of meritorious service." Congratulated by the *Torquay Times*, this was Capt. Read's reply : " No one knows better than I do what a terrific amount of work some people have done, and I would have wished that this honour might have been shared among them. That is not possible, but I hope the fact that the Battalion has been ' recognised ' will give pleasure to everyone. After all, that is what it amounts to, for I shall cherish the honour in the name of the 10th Battalion rather than in my own."

" 1066 and all that ! "

The *Torquay Times* in November 1941 submitted the following to the Regional Censor as part of the Home Guard Notes which that newspaper then featured :

If any Home Guard knows how to use a pike, he had better report to his Battalion Adjutant at once. Torquay is among selected units of the H.G. who, the War Office think, may under certain conditions find themselves involved in close order combat. Hence the arrival this week of a lengthy bundle, which proved to contain 60 excellent specimens of this improvised mediaeval weapon, consisting of a sword bayonet permanently fixed on a steel tube.

It is a well-balanced instrument, about as long as a rifle with a fixed bayonet. A special drill, on the lines of that laid down for the bayonet has been evolved.

I gather that a pike-sergeant instructor has not yet been appointed, nor could I confirm a report that certain volunteers, with experience of pig-sticking in India, have asked that Torquay's pike platoon should be mounted !

Believe it or believe it not, but this was censored—and as far as the *Torquay Times* knows it's censored still !

CHAPTER 5

To "A" Company went the "award" of the Delamaine Line, which would have taken one man for every 35 yards!

"A" Company's many duties included

INLAND DEFENCE

"A" COMPANY came into being when on the suggestion of Mr. Winston Churchill, the L.D.V. changed its title to Home Guard. Prior to this it was known as No. I Platoon, "F" Company, Torquay Rural, consisting of four sections commanded as follows :

    Section 1—St. Marychurch and Babbacombe : Capt. F. J. March.
    Section 2—Hele and Barton : Mr. Garnet Hall.
    Section 3—Shiphay and Edginswell : Capt. Codner.
    Section 4—Chelston and Cockington : Mr. Robart.

The first tasks were " to deny to the enemy the use of the following cross roads : Newton Abbot and Edginswell, Barton and Great Hill, Watcombe and Moor Lane ; " to protect the following V.Ps., and destroy any paratroops landing in the vicinity : " Great Hill reservoir, Gallows Gate reservoir, Petitor, Oddicombe and Babbacombe beaches."

The Mayor (Alderman J. W. Gentle) inspecting the Guard of Honour, under Lieut. C. F. Ellis at the 1943 Birthday Parade.

CAPT. T. A. CODNER
O.C. No. I Platoon which, on reorganisation of the battalion, became " A " Coy.

In true military style this was kept in mind the whole time, with duty working out at three night guards per man per week and the news from our Army in France led us to expect hourly invasion.

Alterations in command became somewhat frequent during the first period, Capt. Codner becoming Platoon Commander, seconded by Capt. Hart. No. 2 Section came under Mr. R. J. Eggbeer, No. 3 Mr. F. E. Bartlett, and No. 4 Mr. W. J. Baker. This was the lay-out then up to the time of re-christening by the Prime Minister, after which the platoon became a company and the sections became platoons. This apart, the organisation remained unchanged.

The already mentioned " Delamaine Line " loomed largely in the company's history. This was its first definite operational commitment and entailed weeks of digging. There were weapon pits to be prepared, barbed wire obstructions to be erected, and, since the company was responsible for eleven roads into Torquay, road blocks also figured prominently in the picture.

In November, 1940, Capt. F. J. March took over as Acting-Adjutant at Battalion H.Q., and was succeeded by Mr. F. J. Lander, while in the following May Capt. Codner and Capt. Hart relinquished their appointments, Lieut. F. J. Lander, with Lieut. R. J. Eggbeer as second-in-command (commissions were now being granted) assuming command with the ranks of Major and Captain respectively.

These latter promotions necessitated changes of platoon commanders to :

No. I Platoon ... ... Lt. R. G. Stamp
No. 2 ,, ... Lt. J. A. Powell
No. 3 ,, ... Lt. F. E. Bartlett
No. 4 ,, ... Lt. W. J. Baker

with the respective second-in-commands, Sec. Lieuts. Ellis, Sweetlove, Thompson and Collings. When the company lost the services of Lieut. Stamp and Sec. Lieut. Thompson their places were taken by Sec. Lieuts. Frayn and Warren.

By now the general routine of the battalion had settled down to intensive training as far as it was practicable. Numerous exercises took place with the Regular troops stationed in the area—the Regulars acting as the enemy. On every occasion when the attack came in from the landward side " A " Company bore its initial stages.

The company at this time was called upon to furnish various extra guards, piquets and patrols on the coast at Torquay Harbour, Torbay front, Corbyns Head and Livermead. About this time the Devon General platoon came into " A " Company and took over the defence of the " Delamaine Line " in the Newton Road area, the Gas Company Platoon assuming responsibility for the western end of the inland defences.

In February 1942 the War Office saw fit to introduce compulsory service, this entailing a pile of work and endless patience on the part of the company commander and his second-in-command in enrolling and listening to the many wails and moans of the " none too keen " recruits.

An intake platoon was formed, and this meant other changes among the sub-units. Lieut. Bartlett took over the new platoon with Sec. Lieuts. Sweetlove and Collings to assist, and Nos. 2, 3 and 4 platoons were commanded by Lieuts. Jeffery, Warren and Hooper, with Sec. Lieuts. Crossman, Ward and Williams as the seconds-in-command. The Torbay area suffered 44 air raids, 313 bombs being reported to have fallen, killing 184 civilians and damaging much property. This company was especially well organised to deal with bombing incidents, resulting in an invariable and immediate turn-out by all platoons, giving important and splendid assistance to the Civil Defence and Rescue Squads. Of the 313 bombs, at least 70 fell in this company area in addition to the three enemy planes which crashed in the Sea Front, Watcombe and Teignmouth Road districts. Many unexploded bombs fell in the area causing further guards to be provided and assistance given in evacuating the residents concerned.

MAJOR F. J. LANDER
Succeeded Capt. Codner in command of " A " Company

In February, 1943, Company H.Q. moved from Rock Road Drill Hall to St. Leonard's Hotel, Newton Road, where the Sector Signal Section was also housed. In July, H5. Platoon (G.W.R.) was transferred to this company and, under the command of Lieuts. Lewis and Vallance were the first to become Light A.A. and come under the operational control of 60 A.A. Brigade.

A mobile striking force was formed about this time, consisting of a detachment of " A " and " B " Companies, and were specially trained as such under the command of Capt. R. J. Eggbeer, fitting in with the revised operational roll of Centres of Resistance, rather than the " Delamaine Line " scheme. It is interesting to note that at one time this latter scheme worked out at one man for every 35 yards of the " Delamaine Line," which was not quite compatible with the principle of " defence in depth " !

Early in 1944 Major Lander resigned to take up another appointment. Capt. Eggbeer became company commander with Lieut. Warren as his second-in-command with ranks of Major and Captain respectively. Lieut. Ward became platoon commander A3., and Sgt. McMorran (as Sec. Lieut.) was appointed second-in-command.

Four names, Capt. F. J. Bennett (Company M.O.), C.S.M. Mayfield, C.Q.M.S. Everdell (everybody's friend and helpmeet) and Cpl. C. T. Coysh (Company Clerk) must be placed on record. All through the history of this company these four have worked behind

MAJOR R. J. EGGBEER
"A" Company's final O.C.

the scenes, so to speak, in a highly commendable way.

Two certificates of meritorious service were gained by Sgts. Godbeer and Coast.

During the latter period of the Battalion's life several prize shoots had been arranged for its many types of weapons and out of the six companies of the battalion, 16 of the personnel of " A " Company obtained first prizes.

The first and last battalion casualties due to enemy action were members of " A " Company— Capt. (then Lieut.) Warren being the first, and Pte. Jonas the last.

No history of " A " Company would be complete without reference to the members of the Wardens' Service, who took advantage of the opportunity given them in 1942/3 by the War Office and the Ministry of Home Security to join the Home Guard.

Early in February these men were enlisted and commenced their training at Shiphay Grammar School with " A " Company's Intake Platoon. Two parades a week were held and the attendance was good ; a modified recruits' course was given, and the platoon, containing as it did many old soldiers, and being composed solely of volunteers, made rapid progress. In due course they were " passed out " and after some discussion as to the best subsequent organisation, they were posted as a separate Civil Defence Section to A3. Platoon.

By now the section had its own N.C.Os, and particular credit is due to Sergt. C. D. Nickels and Corpl. H. Sowden for their excellent work. The original number had been somewhat reduced, partly by call-ups, partly by sickness, and partly by an increase in C.D. duties, but a steady parade of about 20 all ranks was maintained. Younger members were given training with the battle squad, while the older ones spent most of their time with machine guns or antitank guns. All were exercised on the ranges (rifle, miniature, and grenade) and some, notably Sergt. Nickels, L/Cpl. Wyatt and Pte. Walton gave a good account of themselves. Some of the N.C.Os. and a few others went out to the battle ranges on the moors.

Quite apart however from any potential value that the C.D. members (who, incidentally, were under Sec. Lieut. J. W. J. Raikes) might have been to the platoon, the formation of the C.D. Section resulted in such close contact between the two bodies that the result could not fail to have had most beneficial results had the Defence Organisation of the town been really put to the test. It was an experiment in co-operation well worth the time and trouble spent upon it.

CHAPTER 6

When it comes to stories, "A" Company has some first-class raconteurs—as witness these examples of their products.

"A" Company recalls some

MEMORABLE NIGHTS

HIGHWAY patrols became the nightly lot of a number of us during the first winter of our existence and I found it a tactful and diplomatic job dealing with the drivers whom we were obliged to stop. Some were obliging—others truculent and the remainder non-commital. Two or three recollections spring to mind.

The first is that of a full-blown major. Time about 0130 hours. He was driven by a captain in his own regiment. The sergeant in charge of the H.G. patrol was a solicitor by profession. The major was a little "lit up." He had had about seven and a half over the eight and had the misfortune to have left his identity certificate at home. He was courteously directed into the side of the road where he refused to give any details concerning himself and especially his station, on the ground that "a senior British officer could not be asked any question concerning the whereabouts of his unit." He raved and stormed and passed a lot of derogatory remarks about the Home Guard and abuse of a little authority and so on and finally challenged the sergeant in charge of the patrol as to his authority to detain him. At once he was referred to the necessary authority and gently and firmly informed that he was not going to depart until he had disclosed his station and, finally, owing to his conduct, an armed sentry was put over the car and the risks of trying to "run the gauntlet" explained to him. It was hinted to him that the sentry was an old Bisley competitor. When his ardour had cooled (which took about half an hour) a few moments' quiet conversation with the captain cleared the matter up and the stormy petrel was allowed to depart with the little sage counsel that if he "got fresh" with the sentry at the next road block he was likely to meet further adventure !

He was followed by a full-blown Admiral complete with armed outriders. He pulled up at once and produced his card, asking us whether we didn't think "he was a handsome-looking ——."

Before morning a Sergt.-Pilot in the R.A.F. was being driven in the back of an open car, roaring drunk, and produced his card with some very complimentary remarks about the Home Guard, remarking that he thought we were a —— lot of fine fellows and doing a —— fine job. *In vino veritas* !

W.R.A.

★ ★ ★

The falling-off in strength caused by the continued resignation of the elderly men, who found that while the spirit was willing, they could not stand up to the now fairly severe training, and the greater calls on the young men for the Armed Forces left the Home Guard sadly under-manned. Definite duties had to be performed and the need was urgent. The Government in their wisdom therefore adopted compulsory enrolment in the H.G., this being done through the Ministry of Labour.

The 10th Battalion, and therefore " A " Company, was called upon to deal with the men thus enrolled. A serious difficulty arose. A body of more or less willing men was coming in, absolutely untrained, to be mixed at once with the fully trained. This could never work, so the suggestion was made that the recruits should be placed in a training platoon—there to remain for a month or two, get well trained in the use of arms and foot drill, and then be posted to the regular platoons.

As one who had had experience in the formation of a platoon, and who perhaps understood the initial difficulties, I was asked if I would be willing to be transferred from the command of A3. to the new " Intake." To this I agreed with much heart searching. I was leaving tried and trusted comrades—men for whom I had acquired affection and respect, to take over a post which I felt had little pleasure in it. I had always dealt with volunteers—what should I deal with now, under the compulsory enrolment ?

A general view of the Smith-gun and machine gun teams at the Recreation Ground (1943).

A2. Platoon's Smith-gun team, under Sgt. A. Mohan, which won the Battalion shoot at St. Mary's Bay, Brixham, in 1940.

To assist me in this task Lieut. J. Collings was posted as second-in-command. Here for a start was a keen, loyal and efficient colleague. I cannot pay him too high a tribute, and we worked together in perfect harmony. The next step was to secure efficient instructors. The company was combed for N.C.Os. who could tackle this difficult task, and we secured Sergeants Seaman, Heafy and Screech; ideal men for the job. I have been an instructor of sorts all my life, but I take off my hat to these able, loyal sergeants. To see Dick Seaman handle a squad of raw recruits was a revelation. After a short time Sgt. Heafy left for Ireland and his place was taken by C.S.M. Mayfield.

Thus the organisation was complete. Now to enrol the men whom the Ministry of Labour might send.

This was done on certain evenings at the Old Town Hall, and this prosaic task was not without its lighter side. There was some " digging in of toes " when they were asked, " You understand you are subject to Military Law ? " One good man demanded to be examined by the H.G. M.O. *before* he enrolled—in other words he wished to avail himself of the privileges of the H.G. but was unwilling to enrol. He eventually refused to sign. He was not the only one. Such folk were dealt with by the Ministry of Labour and Police.

Thus was the Intake Platoon fed with recruits. Hard cases, some ; unwilling, many ; unlikely to make soldiers, just a few.

The platoon was run in groups based on progress. Some never passed beyond the initial stage. They always had either two left or two right feet ; never one of each—at least so it seemed when it came to foot drill !

A1. Platoon challengers, who beat all comers in the competition they sponsored on the rifle range at the end of 1944.

As the men became trained they were tested by O.C. Company, and if fit posted to various platoons. After about twelve months the supply of " intake " recruits began to dwindle, and the platoon was nearing its end, when ill health forced me to resign my commission, after nearly four years with the Home Guard.

FRED E. BARTLETT.

★ ★ ★

This is the story of a " crisis." On one particular night, in 1941 I think it was, No. I Section of A1. Platoon was doing all-night duty at Babbacombe. The personnel of the guard were enjoying a friendly game of cards in the beach cafe, which was used as a guardroom, with the exception of Pte. Brown, who was on sentry go outside. The alarm bell rang. Out turned the guard. The N.C.O. in charge—five feet nothing in height—flew up the steps, donning his steel topee and shouting to his men " to stand to " on the verandah.

Conversation was excited. " Hi, you've got my tin hat. Where's my rifle ? Do us fix bayonets ? What about the money and cards ? "

" Come on, you fellers. Get a move on," requested the sergeant in terms that brooked no further delay.

By the time all had turned out the N.C.O. had interrogated the sentry. The latter made his verbal report : " I distinctly heard a boat grating over the rock, and heard voices which did not seem to me to be English, but were of a foreign accent. A dog barked, and lights flashed, over there, sergeant," the sentry pointing towards Watcombe. This was serious, to be sure.

The sergeant rushed to phone " Higher Authorities."

"Who the hell has pinched the electric bulb ? Who's got a torch ?" he demanded. One of the party produced a match. By the time the N.C.O. had found a number to dial, the owner of the matches found that his box was almost empty, and on the ground were about 25 short-end matchsticks. Anyway, it was a means of finding a telephone number.

"This must be the number, strike another match while I dial—what did I say the number was ?—444611—yes, that's right . ... Hullo ! Hullo ! could I speak to Lieut. —— ? He's not there ? Where can I get him ? It's urgent. Did you say the club ? Thanks. I'll try there. Goodnight."

More matches, more short ends on the floor. "Well, well, I have got my torch in my haversack all the time," said the sergeant. "Now we can find some phone numbers. Here you are, let's get on to him—what is the number ? 87643—87643, that's it. Eight, seven, six, four, three . ... I'll bet he's gone to bed . ... "

"Hullo 8, 7, 6, 4, 3 ? hullo, hullo—What the hell's wrong with this phone ? Ah ! that's better. Hullo, I've been trying to get the O.C. Pte. Brown has heard boats landing at Watcombe, a lot of foreign talk, dogs barking and lights flashing. Will you deal with it, and get in touch with the O.C. ? Sorry, old man, to get you out of bed."

The one at the other end got busy, for a "fighting party" mustered at Platoon HQ. in the space of a few minutes.

Another photograph from "way back." An A3. Platoon conference in the early summer of 1940.

Orders were issued for cars to be brought, and almost before one could say " Jack Robinson," away went the convoy section to Babbacombe Beach.

Along the Downs Road and down the steep hill. Everything was in a commotion, sentries here, there, and everywhere, and the sergeant giving orders galore. Interrogation followed, but the private persisted in the accuracy of his keen ears and eyes ! So, after a short Council of War, a plan of action was decided. " To Watcombe we go—but mind the mines."

Away go the cars with the fighting patrol to the Military Hospital entrance at Watcombe. After making enquiries at the house for the whereabouts of the Regular Army O.P. somewhere in the grounds, correct directions were received and an approach made to the post. Everything all quiet, not a sound, except the waves washing on the beach below. Arrived at the entrance to the post. It contained no life.

" Anybody here ? " Surprisingly there came a reply, followed by a man rubbing his eyes with one hand and carrying a rifle with the other.

" Have you heard anything of . . . . ? "

" No, Sir, not a thing. It's been a quiet night, but we'll ask the corporal," replied the regular.

The corporal in a vexed and irritated tone confirmed : " There've been no boats puttin' in yer tonight, nor any other night fer that, and us 'aven't 'eard any furrin voices neither."

The corporal, we judged, was still between his blankets, for he did not show himself outside the hut. And it was not long before some of us were seeking the same solace, though if it's an explanation you're looking for your guess is as good as mine. These were early days and lacking the military discipline and training that were due to follow, enthusiasm was the preliminary of many a promising situation.

This was not the least of them.

C. F. ELLIS.

WHAT ! NO MORNING TEA ?
(A True Story)

I think we shall always remember those nights and days spent at Gallows Gate and elsewhere. You remember how we met armed with sticks and one sporting-gun, and how, about August 1940, rifles were issued, and then uniforms ?

Equipment was issued in instalments, usually at Sunday morning parades, and scarcely a Sabbath passed but we received a " prize " in the shape of some part, large or small, of our L.D.V. regalia.

Towards the end of that August I had a slight attack of 'flu,

We were expecting an issue of army boots and sent word to Sgt. " X " that I could not attend parade but that I took size 7. This happened to be the same size as the sergeant's.

Now our route to our Assembly Point or Parade Ground was a very pleasant one, along a valley and across two meadows. That August Sunday morn. Sgt. " X " discovered a ring of mushrooms. Carefully he " camouflaged " his find, and proceeded to the parade to draw two pairs of size seven army boots. Returning homewards, the mushroom harvest was safely gathered in the sergeant's boots. Ten minutes later he called to inquire of the patient's condition and to leave one pair size 7 A.A.

Reassured concerning the health of his promising private, our sergeant took his leave (and the empty pair of boots) with him.

After nearly five years' army experience from 14 to 18, I was charmed with the new service wherein the sergeant delivers new boots to the private—and (consciously or otherwise) freshly gathered mushrooms into the bargain !

" I."

DID YOU KNOW THAT :

A4. Platoon (then L.D.V.) did the first guard at Corbyns Head in June 1940 ?

,, (Infantry) for several months provided a gun crew at Corbyns Battery ; also that this crew whitewashed the gun pit and themselves, and, in addition, made the best " shoot " at Brixham against the rest of battalion gunners ?

,, held the higest percentage of proficiency badges in the Battalion ?

,, won prizes in all Battalion sports—including battle squad race ?

,, won the battalion " pont to point " race ?

,, had two Boer War veterans—C.Q.M.S. Everdell and Cpl. Norris ?

,, were first on the scene, and rescued the pilot and air gunner of crashed aircraft and rendered first-aid ?

,, had two Platoon H.Qs., being favoured first with the Drum Inn, and then the Haywain ?

S. E. HOOPER.

I F

(With apologies to Kipling, and dedicated to A3.)

If you can keep in step, when all behind you
Are changing theirs, and blaming it on you,
If you clean your gun, when all they find you
Is one small, tiny piece of " four by two."
If you can march and not be tired of marching,
Do " Night Patrol " and then your daily task,
With " Yes, Sir, Coming," when your back is breaking,
And answer every query which they ask.

If you can read a map and all that's in it,
Steer straight without a compass, map or star,
Read Semaphore and Morse, eight words a minute,
And spot a Dornier or Heinkel from afar,
If you can strip a Browning Automatic,
And re-assemble it with all parts right,
If you know everything that's symptomatic,
Of Mustard, Chlorine, " X," and Lewisite,

If you can run a mile and not regret it,
If you can hit the bull with ne'er a miss,
Score higher than the sergeant, and forget it,
And never hesitate with " That or This ? "
If you can triumph in unarmed combat,
And face a tank with bomb in lieu of gun,
If you can out-commando the commandos,
You'll may-be get a corp'ral's stripe, my son.

" I."

CHAPTER 7

Meadfoot, Ansteys Cove, Walls Hill and Hope's Nose are never-to-be-forgotten names to "B" Company fatigue parties!

To "B" Company went the task of

GUARDING THE COAST

IT has been found difficult to set down the early history of " B " Company in anything like exact chronological order, owing to the frequent changes of command in the first few weeks, lack of records, and changes in the operational role which caused the personnel to dig their way not only round the coast but half way round the inland perimeter of Torquay as well !

Probably the early night patrols and this pioneer work, directed by heaven knows who, are the outstanding memory of most of them. " Theirs not to reason why, theirs but to dig—or die " was their slogan, and many times they cursed the constantly changing edicts as various Brass Hats toured the area and scrapped everything the last one had ordered.

No-one whose duty—and privilege—it was to serve with " B " Company will ever complain that life was dull. For one thing there never seemed time. Before complaints could develop there invariably came an order either to dig, or to " pick 'em up " and move on to new territory, leaving carefully constructed strong-points behind for somebody else to occupy !

Yes, there was variety in plenty and if an unofficial record had been maintained not merely of the routine spade work of the company but—to add colour to the narrative—of the views of those who did it, this would certainly take its place among the best sellers of our time ! The early log-books, for instance, though adding nothing to our literature, contained many a gem of unconscious humour, many a howler, and (for those who regarded the volume as the one place in which they could express themselves with safety) not a few pious hopes that the stream of " bright ideas " which poured so freely from the Higher Ups would one day be exhausted.

However, for the authentic history of the company we rely on Major R. P. Williams, and his predecessor, Major H. R. Gwennap Moore, C.B.E., thanks to whom we have gleaned the following facts.

" B " Company began life as No. 2 Platoon of " F " Company, Devon L.D.V., on 19th May, 1940, when, having obeyed a summons

Capt. H. R. G. MOORE, C.B.E. R.N. (retd.) Former (and memorable) O.C. "B" Company

to the local Police Station, the following found themselves appointed as Platoon Officers :—

Platoon Commander, Major E. W. K. Bennett.
Alternative Commander, Lt.-Col. E. M. Dunsford.
Platoon second-in-command, Lt. R. P. Williams, R.N. (ret.)
Alternative second-in-command, Capt. J. Brady.

The Company, which was to cover the area of " F " Division Devon Constabulary, was to be commanded by Lt.-Col. Despard Davies, who instructed the above residents that the platoon area of responsibility and for recruiting purposes would be the wards of Babbacombe, Ellacombe, Torre, Waldon, Strand and Torwood, handed them an enormous pile of applications for membership of the L.D.V., and told them to get on and organise the platoon, select suitable posts for sea observation and report back.

Work commenced then and there in the Court Room. Four section areas were decided upon, the application forms sorted on a territorial basis and from these a selection was made of likely leaders who were immediately summoned to report at the Police Station. After interview the following were appointed :

No. 5 Section, strength	97	Lt. W. E. Barnett
No. 6 " "	124	Lt. B. T. Wilson
No. 7 " "	81	Lt. S. G. Davis, M.M.
No. 8 " "	125	Lt. E. R. Winship, M.C

Alternative Leader :
No. 5 Section	Lt. D. R. G. Jones
No. 6 Section	Capt. C. R. Dampier
No. 7 Section	Lt. J. H. Parry
No. 8 Section	Lt. T. R. Lewis

It should be noted here that the reason for the duplication of leaders throughout the organisation was the conception of the L.D.V. as a part time force in which the leaders would take duty turn and turn about.

The next step was the enrolment of volunteers, the contacting of their men by section leaders and then formation into groups for patrol purposes.

By this time the positions on the Thatcher Estate, Hopes Nose and Walls Hill had been selected as platoon observation posts, and night and day patrols continued in various forms without intermission until late in 1943.

In these early days the four sections took duty alternately at the two posts, patrolling from Meadfoot Beach to the north end of Walls Hill, and contacting detachments of Regular troops who manned static defences at Anstey's Cove, Redgate and Meadfoot beaches. Armed with a few rifles which were passed over from patrol to patrol, they had no guard houses, and relieved one another direct from their homes by relays of cars arranged somehow or other by their group leaders. Be it noted, however, that a late relief was practically an unknown event, and, due to the enthusiasm of the volunteers, patrols were more often than not over strength. Among early group leaders appeared such names as Adams, Graham, Lesley, Lidstone, Revill and Noyes, of whom more was to be heard later, and a day man, a volunteer named Moore, from whom H.Q. received, in written "submissions," many trenchant criticisms and constructive suggestions.

MAJOR R. P. WILLIAMS
Second-in-command to Maj. Moore, whom he succeeded in 1942

Meanwhile the construction of defence posts began, but faltered owing to changes in command. Major Bennett handed over to Lt. Bartlett, who re-joined the Army soon afterwards, being succeeded by Mr. Guy who, after a week's furious energy, departed to Company H.Q. as Adjutant, and handed over on 18th July to Capt. H. R. Gwennap Moore, C.B.E., R.N. (retired).

This doughty mariner immediately set up his headquarters in a room at Shenley, Ash Hill Road (kindly lent by Capt. Westmacott, R.N.), impressed as H.Q. staff a very willing family and band of friends, and the shape of things to come began to emerge in outline. In a short time his breezy personality and contagious enthusiasm infected all ranks ; the construction of posts and siting of road blocks proceeded apace, action stations were allotted to every man and call-out systems devised and, by the time sufficient arms had arrived to equip most of the men, a thin red line of posts along our coast line was ready to defy any Hun who dared set foot upon it.

From these beginnings developed the action stations which were to be the scene of their labours for the next two and a half years, and meantime the platoon became a company with the graduation of the L.D.V. into the Home Guard and the sections were organised as platoons.

Company H.Q. was at Wellswood House Hotel with advanced H.Q. at The Moorings, Higher Lincombe Road ; No. 7 Platoon (afterwards B3.) was responsible for the coast from "London Bridge" to the centre of Meadfoot Beach with H.Q. at Meadhurst Hotel, Meadfoot Cross ; No. 5 Platoon (afterwards B1.) was responsible for the coast from the centre of Meadfoot Beach to Bishops Walk, with H.Q. at Kent's Cavern ; No. 6 Platoon (afterwards B2.) took over the coast from Bishop's Walk to the north end of Walls Hill, with H.Q. at Scouts Hut, Walls Hill Quarry ; and No. 8 Platoon (afterwards B4.), at first in reserve, subsequently held the coast line from Marine Spa to "London Bridge" with H.Q. at the Imperial Hotel, then the "Delamaine Line," from Petitor to Shiphay Bridge, with H.Q. at St. Marychurch Vicarage—a very thin red line this—and finally the coast from the north end of Walls Hill to Petitor Point with H.Q. at the Grange, Babbacombe Downs, and later at the Globe Hotel.

The general set-up of the company was as follows :—

O.C. Company, Major H. R. Gwennap Moore, C.B.E.
Second-in-command, Capt. R. P. Williams
C.S.M., A. C. Halahan, O.B.E.
C.Q.M.S., J. Brady
O.C. 5 Platoon (B1.), Lt. D. R. G. Jones
Second-in-command, Sec. Lieut. A. E. O. Brown, M.C. (succeeded later by Sec. Lieut. Graham, succeeded by Sec. Lieut. W. Adams)
O.C. 6 Platoon (B2.), Lieut. B. T. Wilson
Second-in-command, Sec. Lieut. C. R. Dampier
O.C. 7 Platoon (B3.), Lieut. S. G. Davis, M.M. (succeeded by Lieut. A. E. O. Brown, M.C.)
Second-in-command, Sec. Lieut. Larke (succeeded by Sec. Lieut. E. J. Hannaford
O.C. 8 Platoon (B4.), Lieut. E. H. Shambrook (succeeded by Lieut. R. R. Wellman and later by Lieut. O. C. B. Lesley)
Second-in-command, Sec. Lieut. Tucker (succeeded in turn by Sec. Lieut. Wellman, Sec. Lieut. Lesley and Sec. Lieut. G. W. Matthews).

In the earliest stages, being almost unarmed, the role was one of observation and report. As arms became available, to this role was added one of defence, and gradually our own system of communication was set up. All this with the training of men in the use of their weapons, in a unit over 400 strong was a matter demanding

A very wet Sunday afternoon in 1942—the Mayor (Ald. R. J. Bulleid) inspecting B2. Platoon at the Battalion Parade at Torre Abbey Meadows.

The mysteriously formidable "drain pipe" we knew as a Northover Projector—B4. Platoon, exponents of this field piece, take cover from view in an exercise in November, 1942.

no mean effort of organisation, glimpses of which are seen in a contribution from Major Moore.

The steady build-up was seen in the promotion from armlets to denim suits in July 1940, the arrival of 200 rifles in August, the issue of hand grenades and four Browning Machine Guns in September, nine Browning Automatics in October, and four Lewis Guns in November.

It is worthy of note that during September the first parade as a complete unit was held at Ilsham Valley Playing Fields when, out of a strength of 427, four hundred men paraded.

Later on came a static "flame thrower" and "sub-artillery" in the shape of two Northovers, a Spigot Mortar and two Smith Guns.

★ ★ ★

Of the early period Major Moore writes as follows :—

"'B' Company should have Thatcher Post and Walls Hill inscribed in their epitaph, so clearly do these two points stand out in company history, with Oddicombe an interesting third. What difficulties there were, workers and slackers, know-alls and know-noughts ; but under the crust an intense eagerness to be effective. Gradually through individual initiative these posts became equipped with some semblance to the requirements.

"As time went on units of the Regular army super-wired our beaches and sea walls, obstructions were placed in position at the likely landing places and mines were laid.

"Our mobile B.M.G. mounted inside Shambrook's van with Dale in charge became the bugbear of Regular units opposing us in operational exercises. Dale knows every twist, corner and short cut in the district. Many a time he and his crew by-passed attacking " enemy " troops, flung open the back of the van and let fly a burst or two, stepped on it and disappeared to wait, make and take the next opportunity.

" Looking back on it now in the light of enhanced knowledge, most of our early company operational exercises were really good value. It is interesting to record that in July 1941 at a ' post-mortem ' at Company H.Q. on an operational exercise with Regular troops, an officer of the Oxford and Buckinghamshire Light Infantry emphatically declared, ' The H.G. were too strong for us everywhere.'

" But let us hark back to the night watches above Hopes Nose, patrols on Meadfoot, Marine Drive, Bishops Walk, Ansteys, Walls Hill and the Oddicombe Guard. ' B ' Company had more of night duties than any unit in the battalion, but it helped us all to a fuller sense of responsibility and put a keen edge on our soldiering. Many incidents occurred, especially with the occupants of private cars who objected to being moved on and the trouble was that the H.G. had no legal authority to close the Marine Drive and Ansteys Cove Road to night traffic despite the fact that enemy agents could easily be landed during the hours of darkness by boat. When on several occasions in summer cars stayed out all night in a bay on the road a desperate appeal to higher authority eventually won the day and our patrol area was officially closed to through traffic.

" On two occasions in 1940 enemy ' E ' boats, or possibly ' U ' boats, endeavoured, we thought, to draw our fire. Their method of attack took the form of exposing a variety of lights close inshore for a few seconds and then moving rapidly to another close-in position and repeating the performance—Verey lights fired horizontally, a globular pink light and sundry white and coloured flashes. We couldn't make out the slightest sign of a vessel of any type in the murky darkness, but down from Thatcher Post, close to Hopes Nose and under a lee rock, we clearly heard the engines of departing enemy craft. Incidents such as this, and the night we heard the first flight of German bombers streaking down-Channel to attack a Western port, taught us to make cover available against possible promiscuous bombardment from sea or air.

" Mr. Whitley, of Kilmorie, himself an L.D.V. for a short period, very kindly placed a guardroom at our disposal and in November 1940 he lent us a gardener's cottage which, although half a mile out of touch with Thatcher Post, was a very great boon to Nos. 5 and 7 Platoons.

" The Scouts hut at Walls Hill and the beach at Oddicombe also provided much shelter, accommodation and comfort for arms and inner man on the cold and boisterous winter nights when reliefs were ' standing by.' Many a succulent, frizzling hot dish of ' surplus ' from a well known butcher's shop caught the green eye of the Night Visiting Officer while supping a cup kindly proferred by the sergeant or corporal of the Oddicombe Guard !

" Walls Hill saw many war-time happenings out to sea and was more closely concerned with the effects of the ' tip and run ' raids than our other posts.

" The frequent night raids on Portland and Weymouth in 1940, forty miles distant across Lyme Bay to the east, were harrowingly spectacular on some occasions and a horrific flaming sky twenty-five miles overland to the west signified with the sudden flashes of exploding bombs and ack-ack that another western port was being sorely wounded, albeit undismayed and ever determined to show that Westcountrymen can 'take it.' "

On Major Moore's departure from the district in September, 1942, Capt. Williams was promoted to the command of the company and Lieut. R. R. Wellman, promoted to captain and second-in-command, turned over command of B4. Platoon to Lieut. O. C. B. Lesley with Sec. Lieut. Matthews as second-in-command.

This period is chiefly notable for the intensification of training in all branches, and of exercises on a large scale with Regular troops. You will not have forgotten the Hawkins Exercise, in which " B " Company put up a very creditable performance—a patrol of B4. under Sergt. Dale penetrating to the enemy transport lines during the night, while another under Cpl. H. A. T. Coles succeeded in putting out of action a 25-pounder with a " sticky," and getting away intact. There was also the little matter of the triumphant capture of the enemy's cooks and trucks by B2. with its " debagging " sequel in the Scouts Hut when the prisoners showed fight !

Enemy action from the air also became more frequent and many

B1. and B4. Platoons in Camp at Waterside, 1943.

were the " incidents " in which the company was able to render assistance to the Civil Defence.

During 1943 it was decided to train a mobile Striking Force in the battalion which could be used to reinforce neighbouring areas in case of enemy parachute raids, and to this end the more active members of all platoons were transferred to B4. Platoon in exchange for its more static members, who were distributed among the remainder. This platoon was organised as two full battle platoons under command of Lieuts. Lesley and Matthews, with Capt. Wellman as Force Commander. The company as a whole also took up new action stations, forming one centre of resistance on Warberry Hill, which was the central keep and included the Battalion H.Q. and Invasion H.Q., and a second centre of resistance at Shiphay designed to deny the enemy the approach through Newton Road.

In the summer of 1942 came conscription for the Home Guard and " B " Company had set up an Intake Platoon (B6.) with H.Q. at Audley Park School, under the command of Lieut. G. H. Lidstone (late Sgt. B4. Platoon), with Sec. Lieut. H. R. W. Greaves as his second-in-command, Sgt. H. V. Morsley (late B2. Platoon) as platoon sergeant, and an able staff of instructors formed of N.C.Os. drawn from all platoons. Sec. Lieut. Greaves left for London in the autumn of 1942 and was succeeded by Sgt. Morsley, who was promoted to Sec. Lieut. as second-in-command and remained with the platoon until shortly before its work was finished in the first week of 1944.

Lieut. Lidstone then took over command of H1. Platoon, which was transferred to " B " Company in 1943. At this time the strength of the company was over 500, but it soon became evident that many medically unfit men had been drafted in under compulsion and this figure was soon reduced.

This year was also notable for the removal of Company H.Q. to Lumsholme, a villa in the Higher Warberry Road, which also became the home of B3. and B5. Platoons, as well as Battalion Signals and the Battalion Gas Officer.

Mention must be made of C.Q.M.S. J. Brady, that master of repartee and of all the mysteries of " Q," to whom all things came alike, whether in the shape of machine guns or pikes, concrete or veils, face. Heaven knows what he must have issued during the four and a half years, nor what heartburning he experienced at gathering it in again !

Lastly, of whom it can only be said that he was the pivot of the whole organisation (as all of his rank should be), comes the gallant C.S.M. (alias Lt.-Col.) A. C. Halahan, O.B.E. From the early days at Shenley to the end his ripe experience has been invaluable. Hardly an hour at Company H.Q. or a parade of any sort had he missed, no piece of armament or bomb that he had not inspected, no record that had escaped his eye. His exact age goes unrecorded, but young in heart and hardy in physique he has given one and all an excellent example of endurance and devotion to duty.

(DON'T) FOLLOW THE LEADER

It was during one of our early exercises that we were detailed to defend the area around Petitor. Our little party had dug in facing Petitor Tip and the enemy's task was to find our position and our strength.

Having made good progress the enemy eventually found that cover was becoming sparse, and the sergeant decided to make a final charge.

Calling " Follow me " in an authoritative bellow he rushed towards the Tip, misjudged the distance, found he couldn't stop—and went right over the edge. " *Don't* follow me," in a rapidly diminishing tremolo, was the last we heard of him as he disappeared among the junk at the bottom !

Cpl. J. POWELL, B4. Platoon.

"I Submit . . . ."

Loophole—an aperture for firing or looking through. "Loopholes should be *easier* . . . . ,"—remarks by Inspecting Officer.

CHAPTER 8

A tip-and-run raid on the Palace Hotel—then an R.A.F. Convalescent Hospital—coincided with a Home Guard exercise.

"B" Company men were killed in

THE PALACE RAID

THE German air attack on Torquay on the wet and misty morning of Sunday, October 25th, 1942, afforded " B " Company, which had occasion to mourn the loss of two of their number, a unique opportunity of rendering real service.

Now that the irksome Censorship restrictions have been removed it can be openly stated that one of the objects of the attack was the Palace Hotel, which was then being used as a R.A.F. Officers' Convalescent Hospital.

At about 1100 hours while the company was carrying out a tactical exercise in the vicinity, five tip-and-run raiders roared over the building, a H.E. bomb extensively damaging one wing and causing a number of casualties among the patients.

B1. Platoon, under the second-in-command, the late Sec. Lieut. H. W. Adams, lost no time in commencing rescue operations and there is no doubt that but for their prompt action many more lives would have been lost in the wreckage on that fateful morning.

For an account of the incident the Editor has selected a contribution which appeared in C.Q.M.S. Brady's history of " B " Company over the signature of Mr. Adams. This reads :

"Two squads were detailed—No. 1 under Sergt. Curtis to reconnoitre Babbacombe Road to the entrance of the hotel, and No. 2 under my command to reconnoitre the hotel grounds. At about 1130 hours No. 2 patrol had reached a point midway on the south side of the tennis courts.

"Suddenly I heard the roar of planes overhead. On looking up I saw two German planes flying side by side at tree-top height making a direct dive at the hotel. I then saw the plane on the left (now slightly in advance of the other) send the bomb direct for the building. It appeared to be coming down on us. I shouted to the patrol to take cover, which they did. Some went to ground, others took shelter in the gymnasium, Cpl. Duncan and I went down where we were standing.

" The bomb landed direct on the hotel about 25 yards from us. Both Cpl. Duncan and I were lifted by blast and carried about 20 yards, Cpl. Duncan landing in the hedge. Fortunately we escaped injuries but received a bad shock. My trip through the air was brought to an end by the gymnasium wall, receiving nothing more than a cut above the eye and a badly bruised shoulder and ribs. I immediately took the responsibility to cancel operational exercise, and gathered the patrol together.

"I then formed rescue squads, leading No. I Squad to the top storey of the building, No. 2 Squad under Cpl. Jowett taking the second storey from the top. On arriving at the top of the building by way of the fire escape, further progress was stopped by debris. In a few moments we had dumped it overboard and gained entrance.

"The first four we rescued were girls, all of whom were seriously injured, having been completely buried by the debris. We brought them down the escape in blankets as we could not use stretchers. In five hours we had uncovered and brought out 15 persons, six girls all alive, nine men, two dead. We put the four worst cases in bed and made them warm and comfortable. One of these had a broken back. I gave orders that they must not be removed until the doctor had seen them.

"The doctor and matron arrived and I handed them over to their care and placed myself and men under their orders. I remained until the sling arrived and removed the bad cases under the doctor's supervision. In the meantime I received information that two men of No. I Section (Ptes. M. W. Weekes and A. Roe) had been killed. I went to the scene of disaster and found them to be beyond human aid. I identified them and covered the bodies, then reported to Incident Officer and waited until the ambulance arrived to remove them."

★ ★ ★

The C.O. had a remarkable escape, and, indeed, it was amazing that greater casualties were not inflicted on the Home Guard. One hundred I.T.W. R.A.F. cadets were taking part in the exercise, and they, too, were operating in the Walls Hill area.

Lt.-Col. Sloggett writes : "A curious example of the working of the sub-conscious mind—or was it premonition ?—occurred in my own case.

"Oliver Johnson, a well-known actor, used to drive me in his car every Sunday. The car was stopped at the entrance to the Palace Hotel, where I told him to wait while I walked down the road to meet Wing Commander Jenner. When I had gone about 100 yards I suddenly thought the car was in the wrong place ; it would be better camouflaged in the Walls Hill Quarry. I walked back and told Oliver to move the car, which he did.

"Five minutes afterwards the Hun planes flew over and dropped their bombs, one of which made a crater on the very spot where the car had been standing.

The Palace Hotel—after the raid.

"Wing Commander Jenner, the Adjutant and I were in the prone position biting the grass and after it was all over, got up covered with dust and debris—but otherwise intact.

"The Home Guards on the exercise behaved splendidly in helping to get the dead and wounded out and we received a very warm letter of thanks from the Air Ministry and War Office and a special mention from the Corps Commander, General Grassett, on the splendid work they had done, which was what he would have expected from such a really good battalion as the 10th (Torbay)."

In addition to Ptes. Weekes and Roe, whose deaths we deeply deplored, 24 R.A.F. officers and three W.A.A.Fs. lost their lives.

WHO WERE THE KINGFISHERS ?

The best sustained secret in " B " Company's history was the identity of certain generous supporters who styled themselves " The Kingfishers." Quite early in the company's existence parcels of comforts mysteriously appeared over-night, accompanied by a crayon drawing of a Kingfisher and the Latin tag " *Ad ignotium ex ignotius*," or, approximately, " To the unknown from the still more unknown."

Men keeping lonely vigil on the coast had reason to be grateful to the Kingfishers and so anxious were Major and Mrs. Moore to express the company's thanks that efforts were made to solve the mystery. Bur no-one ever saw the parcels arrive and to this day the donors are unknown though not forgotten.

"BRITT : OMN."

The sea is her lover, his passion flows
To the far corners of the globe.
Peru and Burma know his tread,
And he has lain in mangrove swamps, and cradled dead.
Clear as crystal is her love
On his return.

Her lover is our earth, whose pulsing veins
Diffuse broad rivers red from rains.
The hills succumb, by channels deft ;
And if the stream, like God, be lost, the fount is left.
Lowly earth—wear laurel leaves
For she you love.

The sky is her lover, again new dressed,
For he, though one, is all the rest.
His doves and eagles fly her will ;
The elements his coherts ; storm or brooding-still.
Fortunate a love indeed,
To see her face !

H.D.

CERTIFICATES OF GOOD SERVICE

Awarded to—			Bn. Part II Orders No.	
Sgt. Harding, W. H.	H5. Pl.		28 Apr. 44	177
„ Seymour, A. G. E.	" C "	Coy.	28 Apr. 44	177
„ Coast, H. J.	" A "	„	2 Jun. 43	133
„ Nickels, J.	" B "	„	2 Jun. 43	133
„ Godbeer, C. E.	" A "	„	8 Jan. 43	114
„ Miller, W. B.	" B "	„	8 Jan. 43	114
C.S.M. Lidstone, N. J.	" D "	„	8 Jan. 43	114
Sgt. Samson, W. H.	" H "	„	24 Jun. 42	82
„ Scott, W. T.	" C "	„	9 Jan. 42	61
Maj. Wood, F.	" C "	„	21 Jun. 44	187
Sgt. MacDonald, H. G.	" HQ."	„	21 Jun. 44	187
„ Wilkinson, P.	" HQ."	„	21 Jun. 44	187

CHAPTER 9

Over-zealousness, according to Capt. R. J. Harris, on whose knowledge we depend, presented the greatest problem of 1940.

Enthusiastic inception of the

PAIGNTON L.D.V.

PAIGNTON Local Defence Volunteers, formed within hours of Mr. Eden's historic appeal, were organised and commanded by Major E. H. Woosley, O.B.E. Since those early days the two companies which ultimately sprang from the enthusiastic, if inexperienced L.D.V. formation, attained a high degree of proficiency, but both will acknowledge the debt they owe to the highly skilled organising ability and expert guidance of the original O.C.

The bringing of order and discipline out of chaos in such an astonishingly short time was an almost unbelievable feat, possible only by a high sense of duty in extreme emergency. In this preliminary and arduous initial build-up the " back room boys " are sometimes insufficiently recognised. Under Major Woosley's patient guidance the clerical volunteers were called on to execute many hours of difficult organising work every day—without any of the glamour and excitement of soldiering, enrolling volunteers

Col. P. W. Thompson (U.S.A.) taking the Salute at the 1944 Birthday Parade

MAJOR E. H. WOOSLEY, O.B.E.
Commanded Paignton L.D.V.s and later " C " Company

and recording their capabilities and inabilities.

The equipment in May and June, 1940, sounds quite fantastic today—lengths of lead piping, chair-legs loaded with lead, aged revolvers with little or no ammunition, shot guns and rook rifles were all called in to play their part in the Great Emergency.

The majority of the early volunteers had previous army experience and all felt the need for immediate training and a measure, at least, of discipline and physical fitness wherever possible. P.T. squads were started at seven o'clock in the morning, even training in drill and musketry instruction was instituted daily in Queen's Park and other centres ; sticks were used in place of rifles, and route marches on Sunday mornings (in civilian dress of course) were well attended.

Such was the spirit of determination and enthusiasm with which Paignton met the threat of invasion.

At length the long-looked-for consignment of rifles arrived from America—direct from Rock Arsenal, Long Island, packed in their moulds of solid grease as they had lain since 1918 ! And then another problem reared its head—how were 60 rifles to be distributed among 200 men ? This accentuated what was perhaps the greatest difficulty underlying the whole administration and control of the Paignton L.D.V.—over-zealousness. Yet should it be called an unqualified difficulty ? In reality such over-zealousness was but the expression of extreme enthusiasm and determination to deal effectively with the job in hand.

It should be noted here that for the purpose of this " history " we must speak of the " Paignton Home Guard " as " the Paignton L.D.V.", for until the time of compulsory enrolment there was only one company in Paignton, collectively known as " C " Company.

The many stories that might be told of the incidents and comical situations that arose in this most extraordinary of quasi-military forces are sufficient to fill a separate book. The section-commander endeavouring to aid the police to locate an elusive light at midnight on the hill tops ; crawling on hands and knees, shrouded in a ground sheet, among the grazing sheep, hoping and believing that he looked like one of his woolly-coated companions, in a brave effort to stalk the perpetrator of the " elusive light crime." Unfortunately for this enterprising venturer others were also stalking the light in a more normal fashion and, seeing in the moonlight this very extraordinary looking animal with whom the other sheep were obviously not fraternising, were on the verge of believing this to be the " signalling spy " himself—and nearly took action accordingly !

In the face of many obstacles and shortages Paignton struggled along with its training and it is gratifying to recall that much pioneer work and enterprising training methods were produced by this company and shared with others within the battalion. It is believed that the first demonstration squad was conceived, equipped and produced by this company in the anti-tank ambush displays staged between Occombe and Cockington before large numbers of spectators from other sub-units. Home-made smoke generators, token bombs and other " effects " were all made by the personnel of this first demonstration platoon.

MAJOR F. W. GRANSMORE
Major Woosley's successor

With the introduction of compulsory enrolment the company suffered a grievous loss in the resignation of Major Woosley. The command, however, was ably carried on by Major F. Gransmore. Prior to this the company had, by occasion of its great strength, been formed into a " double company "— C1. and C2. This permitted a larger establishment of officers and N.C.Os. and, with the promotion of Major Gransmore to senior major, Capt. E. H. Hopkinson took over command of C2. Company with the rank of major. The company seconds-in-command were Capt. G. Bentley (who had been serving under Major Woosley from the early days of the company's formation) and Capt. F. Wood, who, as senior platoon commander, was promoted second-in-command C2. Company.

Maintaining the Paignton company's tradition for initiative, the suggestion for a special training platoon for the conscripted recruits was adopted throughout the battalion. Considerable use was made of this recruit training platoon in the early days of its existence as a means of affording N.C.Os. throughout the two companies intensive refesher training in drill and man management.

With steadily increasing issues of stores, arms and equipment and the rapid development towards more military discipline and administration, it was found that the very large company—over 800 strong—which was, despite its being a double company, still commanded and administered as one sub-unit from one H.Q. and Stores, was far too unwieldy. The company was therefore split into two distinct companies, the one remaining in the original H.Q. with a task of defending the centre and greater part of the town and beaches, and the other defending a southern section of the town and the outskirts and beaches to the south. For some reason the company commanded by the senior major and remaining in the original H.Q. in the centre of the town, was re-named " F " Company, whereas the other was given the original title of " C " Company.

The command of the newly dissected " C " Company would normally have passed to Major Hopkinson, but he, owing to important business responsibilities, felt unable to accept the appointment. The mantle of company commander therefore fell on the shoulders of Capt. F. Wood, who was forthwith promoted major, while Major Hopkinson reverted to the rank of captain as second-in-command, at his own request.

★ ★ ★

Paymaster Commander A. R. Eversleigh Green, R.N. (retd.)—who ultimately succeeded to the command of the old No. 12 Platoon—dealing with the first few days of hectic activity at Paignton, writes :

It was obvious that N.C.Os. would be necessary and our first job was to select suitable men, divide the section into workable units and put them in charge. We made a lot of mistakes in our choice of men, but our principal difficulty was to find those who had the time to spare (which sounds strange in 1946 ! !). Others there were who, though eminently suitable, declined to take on the responsibility so that in the end we had to take a number of men at their own valuation, which was frequently higher than their performance !

One man (no names of course !) was chosen on account of his soldierly appearance. I kept the records and knew that he had never been a soldier, but he was made an N.C.O.—as I suspected, he knew even less about the job than I did. To give him his due, I could find no fault with his enthusiasm, but in those early days it was experience we needed and very often a man's service record gave a wrong impression as to his ability to take charge.

However, there were certain notable exceptions and I think I may be permitted to single out a few for special mention.

To begin with, it was necessary to find a good drill instructor and in Mr. R. Layfield we found the ideal man. He was large and tough, had been 12 years in the army, most of it as an instructor on the parade ground, and some 22 years in the Metropolitan Police.

Paignton Companies jointly demonstrate their efficiency (in this case in the E-Y rifle and cup discharger) on the Green.

Without him it would have been very hard to make any sort of beginning to turn a miscellaneous collection of civilians into a fighting force. He was a keen and painstaking instructor and quite apart from evening parades, he took a small class of the more active, and perhaps more zealous, in rifle drill at 7 a.m. Mr. Walker (of the Steartfield Garage), who had lent us his premises, also provided us with dummy rifles so that we were able to start arms drill long before American arms were received.

Our next discovery was one who wore the ribbons of both South Africa and Great wars, and must have been about 60 years of age. When he first arrived, he came in a taxi—in fact for some time he was unable to go any distance except in a car.

He proved to be of the utmost value—he volunteered to teach musketry, and although I have been under many instructors in the subject, I learned more from Mr. C. D. J. McLellan than from any previous teacher. Despite his health he was indefatigable—and could turn his hand to almost anything. I cannot speak too highly of his help and support during those difficult times.

Aided by the experienced McLellan, volunteers from the section later built small strong points out of sandbags, tree-trunks, old railway sleepers, corrugated iron and any other material available. It was appreciated that they would never stand up to being bombed but it was hoped that the enemy might overlook them until too late for his health !

The rest of the men were scattered along our long front in small units, with instructions to make use of cover and do their best if invasion came. It was realised that with no field telephones and with the lack of vision from one end of the front to the other, it would be impossible to co-ordinate the efforts of the whole line, and that if the enemy made a landing along both beaches at once, our force was too small to admit of any men being held in reserve, so that our only hope was to " stay put " where we were and fight it out.

From such positions there could be no retreat. I should have liked to have been able to man the sea-wall so as to get a clear view of the beach below, but the army proceeded to wire it so that we could get no view of the beach.

At this time, small detachments of soldiers were stationed in Paignton for periods varying from a week to a fortnight—sometimes we had both soldiers and L.D.Vs. patrolling the sea-front and sometimes we were left to hold the fort by ourselves. The army took over the Cafe de Paris where units followed one another in quick succession. Sometimes it would be full of soldiery and just as we were beginning to know them and achieve some measure of co-operation with them, they would vanish in the night. We managed to persuade one O.C. to let us have an armoury in a small room at the cafe, where the indispensable McLellan set up shop and looked after rifles and, later, machine guns. We decided to set up an

M.G. post on the roof of the cafe as it offered a good field of fire, but it was also damnably open to air attack—a fact that was not popular with those manning it, though they were a stout-hearted lot.

We had been loaned a large and powerful telescope on a stand, and each O.C. in turn was warned that it belonged to us and was asked to keep an eye on it. The troops were permitted to use it so long as they didn't leave it out in the rain, but, alas, after my day there came an O.C. who either failed to receive the warning, or failed to heed, because a year or so later, when the owner of the telescope enquired for it, the soldiery, or perhaps other misguided persons, had made off with all the lenses and left a mere hulk behind.

I cannot leave the L.D.V. without paying a warm tribute to those members of the staff of the Prudential who joined us—they were certainly the backbone of our platoon and when they left Paignton they were sadly missed. If there is one name which leaps to mind it is that of Mr. N. H. McClatchie, who was a tower of strength, and who later followed in my footsteps in command of the platoon.

I should also like to pay a tribute to the memory of Lionel S. Jackson ; he was one of our youngsters and a very willing worker with O.T.C. experience. Later he left to join the R.A.F. and gave his life whilst serving as a sergeant. I hope that his preliminary service in the L.D.V. contributed something to his training.

Another who should be mentioned is the late Sergeant A. W. Geake—a tough old soldier of the last war and a very good fellow.

During holiday times, we were assisted by several public school-boys, mostly O.T.C. members, who were a great help, but it is to the rank and file of everyday Englishmen that the credit of the success of the venture is due. It didn't matter whether a man was a retired Colonel with a D.S.O. or the owner of a small business, or his employee—they all managed to shake down together and in due course became welded together in the ranks of the Home Guard.

And, finally, a cheerful footnote from Lieut. Hill, who recalls the May, 1940, visit to the Police Station " where one's military past came to light after one damn question after another had been asked, answered and duly recorded, and other enrolment had been made for entry into what must have been the world's largest and most unpleasant ' reception committee ' for would-be intruders on the soil of Britain.

" A huge section was soon established on the sea-front and probably never before in the history of Britain have so many Englishmen met each other without being formally introduced !

" Patrols were formed, duties arranged, identity cards very frequently inspected, causing no little annoyance to those who considered themselves known to everybody, but eventually the

The Stoke Gabriel Platoon under Lieut. Herrod march past (1944).

'Watch on the Brine' was being systematically and thoroughly carried out with no thought of shirking or evading responsibility or duty.

"It subsequently transpired that our platoon was under Naval control, both commanders being ex-R.N., and we had to adapt ourselves to Naval terms and orders.

"Watches, not guards, were instituted—but alas not once did we receive the order to 'splice the mainbrace.'"

The ritual of changing the watch, checking identity cards, and the inventory was a real experience, particularly the latter, which revealed at one post that the weapons for immediate use in repelling an invasion were :

Police truncheon	1
Indian clubs	2
Lead piping, plus string	1
Revolvers (private)	?
Rifle	1
Ammo for same (doubtful fit), rounds ...	10

OUR OLD FRIEND "MAC"

This is just one of the scores of stories which can be told of that old war-horse, Mac, of No. 12 Platoon.

What was he like ? Well, if you close your eyes and conjure up a picture of Captain Kettle, minus a beard, that's him. It was a pity he did not sport a beard. He was all shot to pieces and one could never understand how he managed to hold together. He had a limp, a liking for strong ale and a lovely flow of language gathered from all the campaigns of the past fifty odd years.

His age ? Oh, round about three score years and ten. Finally, he was a real two-gun man, with half-a-dozen notches to his credit, and he could throw a slug 200 yards and score a bull.

As you can imagine, such a man was worth his weight in gold. No. 12 never needed any lectures on morale or the offensive spirit.

However, one bright starlit morning, maybe about 0300 hours, young Vol. P—— and not-quite-so-young Vol. F—— were dutifully patrolling the Paignton sea-front, alert for signs of enemy action. The youngest carried the ancient rifle ; his comrade the ammunition—both clips !

They had spent a hectic fifteen minutes trying to pick up and locate the sound of a high-powered motor. Was this the morning ? Was it air-borne or water-borne ? Hell ! No, only the refrigerator in Pelosi's ice-cream hut. Whew ! what next ? Nothing. All is peaceful. In another twenty-five minutes they will be making for the second shelter, where their flasks and sandwiches are snugly reposing.

Oh ! blast. The siren.

Will the darn thing ever stop screeching and give a couple of Churchill's beach fighters a chance to spot the enemy ?

Is this it ?

Gosh, it seems as lonely as the desert here.

" Quiet there, big feet."

" Yes, a plane. Out to sea but flying this way."

" Can you hear it, boy ? "

" Not 'arf I can't."

" What in the hell are we supposed to do ? "

" Keep our eyes skinned, I presume, Senior Volunteer."

" Who the devil is this charging across the green ? Challenge him and no nonsense. I'll keep out of sight."

In the middle distance a figure could be seen, and heard, coming top speed towards the two rather disturbed patrolmen.

At last the challenge : " Halt, who goes . . . "

" Cut out that so-and-so nonsense, who the —— is on duty ? "

(Oh lord, old blood and thunder. What does he want ?)

" Volunteer P—— and Ditto F——, sir."

" Are you armed ? "

" Yes, sir " (proudly).

" Enemy plane. Can you fire that rifle ! "

" Yes, sir."

A short pause.

" Are you loaded then ? "

" No, sir. Not yet."

" Well, do you think you can load ? "

"I think so, sir." (Of course the old blighter was trying to get the only rifle we had into his own hands.)

"You *think* so. Gimme. Don't crowd. Scatter. Smaller target." All the time Jerry droned remorselessly on his way south at about 40,000 feet. Whack, crash, click. Four in the mag. and one up the spout.

"Who's got the other clip ? Gimme."

Eventually silence. But not for long.

"You two. Keep your eyes skinned for parachutists. If you find any, stick your thumbs in their eye-balls." Oh yeah !

At long last even Mac was satisfied that he was out of luck that night.

"Here, you, take the rifle and don't shoot yourself. I'm going back to bed. Good-night."

Phew ! thank goodness for that.

"Come on, let's go and have some food." And a few minutes later two tired sentries were munching well-earned food, in peace.

"Blimey, here he comes again."

"Who ? "

"Old Mac. Give him a real snorter of a challenge."

"Sentry ? " in that rasping voice.

"Yessir."

"I've come back to tell you I dropped the cartridge clip when I was loading earlier on. When it's daylight search the Green for it. Good-night."

"Good-*night*, sir."

E. FRICKER, F2. Platoon.

A happy—and refreshing—moorland interlude. But what was in the Thermos we shall never know !

"INSPECTION INVITED"

CHAPTER 10

Growing strength and administrative difficulties made a "split" inevitable: the result—"C" and "F" Companies.

In 1943 occurred "C" Company's

RE-ORGANISATION

FOLLOWING the division of Paignton's double company, "C" Company, under the command of Major F. Wood, M.S.M., with Capt. E. C. Hopkinson, M.C., as second-in-command, established headquarters at the Goodrington Hotel (where the old 10a Platoon, later known as C4. Platoon, had occupied the ground floor for some 15 months). The inlying piquet, which until then occupied the upper rooms, had to be moved to the Drill Hall, York Road. All liaison with A.R.P., C.D. Services, Police, N.F.S., Fire Guards, Ministry of Labour, the Invasion Committee, Paignton U.D. Council and the W.V.S. was carried out by Sec. Lieut. Ainsworth, whose duty it was to keep both " C " and " F " Companies in close touch with those Services mentioned. The platoons were to be known as :

C1. at "C" Company H.Q.	Sec. Lieut. Burch	
C2. at Roundham area	Lieut. Haddock	
	Sec. Lieut. White	
C3. at Stoke Gabriel	Lieut. Knight	
	Sec. Lieut. Herrod	

Major-General A. G. Arbuthnot, C.M.G., D.S.O., inspecting the "Salute the Soldier" Week Guard of Honour (C5. Platoon) under Lieut. G. Jarvis.

MAJ. E. C. HOPKINSON, M.C.
From second-in-command "C" 2 Company, became O.C. on Major Gransmore taking over command of "C" I

C4. at Ciennon Hill area   Lieut. Grainger
                                         Sec. Lieut. Mugford
C5. at Waterside area   Lieut. Hicks
                                           Sec. Lieut. Jarvis
C6. at Drill Hall   Lieut. King
                                           Sec. Lieut. Underhay

Capt. H. Clark was to be Company Medical Officer; the C.S.M. was R. S. Lake, M.M., and the C.Q.M.S. H. Tomlin, who had his stores in the South Sands Cafe.

About the middle of January 1943 anti-aircraft guns were located around Torbay, and in order to accommodate the crew of the gun on the headland at Three Beaches, C5. Platoon were turned out of their hutments almost at an hour's notice, and so " Seafield House " was requisitioned a few days later, actually during the sale of the contents and property on 25th January, 1943.

From then onwards C5. Platoon settled into comfortable quarters having previously been housed in P.U.D.C. huts since the early days of the L.D.V.

During the first week of January, 1944, the company had orders to vacate Goodrington Hotel within seven days and it was decided to transfer to " Seafield House," Waterside. The old St. Michael's Church having been requisitioned for C4. Platoon, the company once again became completely housed. These changes necessitated re-organising the whole of the company's operational role and in a short time platoons soon settled down again in their new fighting positions. As " D " Day approached " C " Company did its full share of guards at the V.P., Brixham, and when the order came for all compulsory parades to cease, Company and C5. Platoon H.Q. were transferred to the Drill Hall, York Road.

The only change in officers since " C " was made a separate company was the resignation of Lieut. King (C6. Platoon), who was succeeded by Lieut. Mugford of C4.; and Sergt. N. Heeks' promotion to second-in-command of C4, vice Lieut. Mugford transferred.

COMBINED OPERATIONS ?

It was a night exercise to test the speed which information of a coastal landing might with luck reach Battalion HQ. and the enemy were represented by small craft of the Royal Navy.

On the coast straining ears and drowsy eyes made unremitting inquiry of the fateful waters of Torbay.

At company headquarters the idle hours went by in stories

good and stories bad and with the sardonic humour with which generations of soldiers have sought to relieve in trench or billet the boredom of campaign.

At length the telephone rang and an outlying post reported : " Can hear boats and horrible language at sea."

Rapidly this was repeated to Torquay, with the addition " Whether hostile or friendly not yet known."

The post was contacted and the exact details of the language imperatively demanded. Company headquarters felt they were missing something good. Back came the reply : " We heard someone shout, ' Get out of my way, you ——.' "

Doubts no longer existed. No question of identity. It was obvious. Battalion were informed, " The Royal Navy are off G beach." They had run true to form and once again " It was upon the Royal Navy and under the Providence of God that the safety of this Realm chiefly depends."

MAJOR F. WOOD, M.S.M.
Second-in-command of " C " 2 under Major Hopkinson and then O.C. " C " Company

E. C. H.

NIGHT GUARD IMPRESSIONS, 1941

He had fallen into a reverie and his actions were automatic as he forced his tired limbs to climb the high bank, his " civvy " socks damping in his army boots as he trudged through the long grass.

The wind was rising after the early evening rain, the clouds were thinning and the bombers' moon would soon be up.

He gazed to the West, towards Plymouth, and wondered— listening for the drone of the raiders. All quiet—so far. He had had a busy day and he yawned heavily, his body sagging for rest.

Passing the guard hut a burst of laughter made him yearn for its companionship and warmth. With a physical effort he carried on— wondering how long before relief was due.

Down towards the gate he went, great-coat, respirator, anti-gas cape, the modern equipment of war weighing heavily on unaccustomed shoulders.

He drew a deep breath, knowing from experience that fresh reserves of energy would return as the night wore on.

Down to the gate—where his pal was doing static " sentry go."

And then . . . the banging of doors and the clatter of gear as the relief sentries turned out.

The distant drone of engines—then the almost simultaneous "alert," the heavy, intermittant groan of enemy planes passing in seemingly endless procession on the now only too familiar route. Searchlights far to the west, the flicker, then the thud of distant bombs, a plane at times pin-pointed in the intersecting shafts of light. . . .

Time passed—time heavy with suppressed anxiety for the distant town. . . . An eerie silence—the "all clear." Tension relaxed—with banter, in fits and starts.

The reliefs had taken over.

He entered the guard hut, eyes stung by the piercing light. Easing his equipment from his shoulders he realized that his tiredness had slipped unknowingly from him.

A cup of tea, his rations, the warmth from the fire—and the cheerful atmosphere of his pals seeped into his being.

His fresh reserves of energy had returned again and he felt as ready and quick-witted as the next for the long night's vigil and the rest of his duty to come.

F. G. W., C2.

Certain of the photographs in this book are reproduced by courtesy of Mr. Herbert F. Canty, whose co-operation is gratefully acknowledged.

"Goodbye to all that"—Major Wood takes leave of his officers at "C" Company's final parade.

CHAPTER 11

From Battle Platoon achievements to their incomparable "Mac," "F" Company is rich in memoirs. Here are just a few samples.

Lost on the Golf Course—or a

NOCTURNE IN F

IF there were one feature of "F" Company's history that predominated it was probably the efficiency of its battle platoon. Other companies are entitled to regard themselves as having been equally fortunate in the choice of personnel, but none had a greater proportion of enthusiasts. And no battle platoon has taken greater pains to secure adequate representation in this book, for contributions by "F" Company's battle platoon members exceed in number and fluency all that has been received from other quarters—and a convincing story they tell !

Lieut. W. H. Harding, O.C. Platoon, who generally acknowledges the high standard attained by the battle platoons of other companies, has provided a reminder of the time when the role of the H.G. was being changed almost daily as the swiftly moving blitzkrieg tactics of the enemy sprang new surprises. Although, as he says, the chief role was then a static one, it was realised that upon the advance information obtained by patrols everything would depend.

These patrols in many cases formed the nuclei of battle platoons.

In "F" Company the battle platoon was a composite body formed of battle squads from various platoons in the company and had not the advantage of continuous training as a complete unit. It was with some gratification, therefore, that in the summer of 1943 they learned they were to provide the demonstration battle platoon for the visit of " T " Travelling Wing.

One of the earliest public appearances of the battle squad as such was as a patrol from No. 14 Section of 12 Platoon " C " Company when the company was taking part in an exercise against Regular troops. The squad succeeded in locating the main attack and getting information back within a matter of seconds by means of flag signals from pre-arranged O.Ps. After contacting and engaging forward elements of the " enemy," this patrol then distinguished itself by passing through the " enemy " lines (in broad daylight), by using its local knowledge, and rejoining its platoon to take part in the final action. One pleasing feature of the operation was noted when the

MAJOR G. F. W. A. BENTLEY
O.C. "F" Company. Formerly second-in-command of "C"

patrol commander located two of his advance scouts (who had been detailed to return by an alternative route) busily reviving two of the enemy whom they had "killed," by means of copious draughts of "medicine" in an adjacent hostelry!

Battle drill, wood-clearing and street-fighting tactics had all been explored and practised for some time before the issue of H.G.I. No. 51, from knowledge gained from friends in the Regular army who had undergone the then new type of training, and much knowledge was also gained from various Home Guard officers who had been fortunate enough to attend courses at "Denbies." It will be remembered that each Army School had its own particular method of laying on battle drill, in consequence of which none could be acclaimed correct.

One memory is of a certain Sunday morning when the whole of No. 12 Platoon paraded in a large field to receive instructions in battle drill, and the spectacle of several officers and sergeants dashing about with sheaves of papers from which they endeavoured to propound the art of "Platoon in attack—right flanking"!

However, with the advent of the official Home Guard Instruction No. 51, battle practice was co-ordinated, but the knowledge previously gained was of inestimable value, and No. 12 Platoon's battle squads were able to demonstrate "how to do it" to other platoons in the company.

Lieut. Harding, in a reference to Sgt. J. C. Bosanko, says : "He has acted as general factotum, and I doubt whether there is a job he had not tackled, ranging from explosives expert to platoon runner. His efforts at beating the clock in the latter capacity had to be seen to be believed, while his expert first-aid knowledge was frequently called into practical use to deal with the many minor casualties, not forgetting his unofficial role as photographer and tame poet to the platoon.

"I would like, too, to express what my fellow N.C.Os. and I often said among ourselves in those uncertain days—that if the "balloon" had really gone up, these were the fellows we wanted to be with—but has not every officer and N.C.O. said exactly the same thing about every H.G. throughout the battalion ?"

★ ★ ★

Sgt. Bosanko is nothing if not versatile. Poems, manuscripts and photographic negatives have reached the Editor in a bewildering succession, but limitations of space forbid more than the following few extracts :

The battle platoon was comprised of men who were mostly young and active and all tireless workers who often did more, much more, than their platoon commander expected.

In company exercises they distinguished themselves, and developing a "multiple prong" technique achieved their object time without number. These tactics, the sergeant modestly affirms, were also used by General Montgomery!

This particular stratagem was notably successful in attacks on Stoke Gabriel and Marldon. In the Marldon show it was a battle platoon member who deliberately became a prisoner to be enabled to "blow up" enemy headquarters, incidentally giving the intelligence people a perfect demonstration that all prisoners should be searched. . . .

How was the "blowing up" accomplished? Well, at this time all "effects" such as thunder flashes, smoke, etc., were practically unobtainable, so battle platoon personnel used expedients of their own. Their chemist was responsible for some original gadgets.

Everyone knows the difficulty of lighting a thunderflash fuse on the armband or loose matchbox, but this was overcome by setting a Swan match in a gum and chlorate "gaine," so arranged that it made part of the fuse extension. Thus a quick "strike anywhere" fuse was made.

Imitation land mines and "step on" booby traps, which anticipated the Hawkins canister, were made with ampoules of acid in conjunction with chlorate attached to standard fuse. The ampoules were originally intended for medicinal fillings!

"Instant" fuse was improvised from firework type quickmatch, and smoke was obtained by the devil's own cocktail of pitch, sulphur and nitre.

Popular Friday night training for the platoon was indoor battle drill. Cpl. Webber made a complete wooden model of a battle

Heil — ? "F" Company's battle platoon which supported "C" Company at "the capture of Stoke Gabriel" in 1943.

squad ; ingeniously arranged by pegs and movable strips each man could be moved at will and the rifle and B.A.R. could be positioned as required. Everyone practised on this and every member could visualize exactly what was happening.

Toggle ropes were in use by the battle platoon long before their general use by H.G. units. Thanks to Sgt. Fricker, who generously provided them, these were tried out before the " T " Travelling Wing came to introduce them !

Wood clearing as a drill was another home-produced effort of this platoon, a drill evolved by Lt. Harding being highly commended and, in fact, adopted by Travelling Wing.

It should be noted that mobile battle squads were active in other platoons in the company and to obtain a composite battle platoon squads from F2., F3. and F5. formed the demonstration platoon, officered by Lt. Boddington. This officer's leadership was an inspiration. He followed the firm battle squad tradition that no officer or N.C.O. should call on any man to do anything that he would not, or could not do himself. Witness this creed in barbed wire crossing drill where the bulkiest N.C.O. became the " laying on" member—or the classic occasion when Lt. Boddington with his one arm did a thirty feet toggle rope climb !

Subsequently the Battle Training School commandant paid the platoon this tribute :

" My duties take me all over the country from Land's End to Carlisle, and I can truthfully say that I have never seen a better Home Guard battle platoon than the one you have been watching this afternoon. It is very gratifying for my instructors to see how well the lessons they have tried to teach you have been assimilated."

Thus was " F " Company's battle platoon officially commended.

One of the most amusing, but so very typical, stories is provided by Major Bentley himself. The incident he describes could have happened to any one of us and probably did in one form or another on those pitch-black nights, when, expecting the worst, we stumbled around, over-eager, perhaps, to do our bit, but very determined to " keep moving." Readers may cast their minds back to incidents like this and smile with Major Bentley at the surprising adventures that befell respectable, middle-aged citizens in the days of the L.D.V.

This is what Major Bentley says :

In 1940 we were constantly receiving word from various sources that lights had been seen at such and such a place, but we did not take any action other than report the matter to the police. The tables were turned, however, on one very foggy November evening

F6. (P.U.D.C.) Platoon's smartly turned-out Smith-gun team attracts attention.

when the police came to Company H.Q. for military advice with a report that a light had been seen in the proximity of the golf links, as though signallers were attempting communication.

Prompt action was necessary, but the only person at Company H.Q., with the exception of the night guard and I, was the company armourer.

Now the armourer is very deaf, but he having assured me that he knew every inch of the ground, I decided he would be a good man to have around.

It was a very foggy November evening and on account of the density we had difficulty in finding our way, but eventually arrived at a spot where we could park the car and from whence we commenced to make our way towards the course.

Arriving there the armourer invited me to place my hand upon his shoulder.

We couldn't see an inch before us, and not knowing the ground I kept a tight hold, but we had not gone far when I felt myself walking up an incline and my hand gradually leaving the shoulder of the guide.

All of a sudden I shot into the air and fell full length into what I thought was a pit, but which I afterwards found out was a bunker.

The guide being deaf I was afraid to shout lest I should give our presence away—so from that time onwards I was minus a guide !

I walked around several times to try and make contact but without avail, so began to go cautiously forward on my own, until I saw a light flash about twenty yards ahead. I moved in that direction, making the usual challenge (revolver in hand) and fell into another bunker . . . . . .

Then I saw another light appear about ten yards to my left, and when I thought I was sufficiently near, yet not being able to see or hear movement, challenged three times. But there was no reply so I decided to give the whole thing up and return to H.Q.

That was easier said than done, as I did not know in which direction to turn. . . . I travelled round and round, falling over more bunkers and coming up against numerous obstacles, including barbed wire, and having lost my torch when I first fell, I had to make the best of it.

Then I decided to follow the wire from which I had just managed to disentangle myself as that would at least save me from going around in circles. Gently tapping the wire with my hand as I slowly went along, I had not gone far when I felt a hand tap the back of mine and a voice ask " Is that you, Capt. ? " I had indeed found my guide, but how he managed to get on to the opposite side of the wire is a mystery !

We decided not to lose each other again, so grabbing hands over the wire we proceeded slowly until brought to a sudden halt by a brick wall which we eventually found was the back of some houses, and at last my guide knew where he was.

From there we soon found our way to the main road and after taking some time to find the spot where we had parked the car in the early hours of the morning arrived back at Company H.Q. feeling that we should both be lucky if we did not have pneumonia, and I being covered from head to feet with sheep, rabbit and other droppings, did not feel in a good temper.

But this was one time when I was thankful for my denims, and the occasion marked my early decision that future cases of unauthorised lighting could be dealt with by the police—and not by the L.D.V. !

Paignton Urban District Council's Platoon (F6.), formed in October, 1940, to protect the Council's property, had as its nucleus Volunteers Bentley, Bowen and Sercombe, who agreed to transfer from No. 9 Platoon, the former being appointed section leader and the first parade being held in the basement of the Finance Department in Totnes Road.

Very soon Vol. Bentley received a company appointment, Vol. Bowen succeeded as section leader, it was decided that future parades be held in Queen's Park, and such was the general desire for efficiency that the platoon, although strictly speaking a " private concern," took part in battalion exercises with real zest, and embarked upon fortnightly camps, the popularity of which was maintained to the end.

" B.A.C." (the platoon's narrator) records that in August, 1941, headquarters were moved to St. Mary's Reservoir at Lammas Lane, platoon strength by now having increased to 26.

Two old stalwarts, Sergts Crouch and Kentispeare, did yeoman work in building up the efficiency of the platoon, and Sergt. William worked assiduously behind the scenes as quartermaster and was rewarded with a commission when appointed second-in-command, and later platoon commander when Lieut. Bowen retired on the advice of the Company Medical Officer.

This promotion brought in its wake that of Sergt. Crouch to commissioned rank, a popular and well-earned reward for untiring and devoted service.

The medical arrangements were in the capable hands of Corpl. P. F. Hart, while the important post of cook was splendidly carried out at all camps by Vol. F. Shute, who was as proud of his cookhouse as any housewife.

Several old members left to join the Army and served in all parts of the globe, one of the best remembered being Vol. Sercombe, the old transport wallah, who was never so happy as when he had his car full of blankets, ammunition or " old crocks."

A word of praise, too, is due to all men who gave unstintingly of their spare time in all weathers to carry out the various duties assigned to them.

May memories of F6. Platoon ever linger.

THE BODY IN THE BAG.

A shadowy form was silhouetted against the breaking surf. The challenge " Halt " rang out and a man stopped. Unable to produce an identity card, he was evidently on a secret mission. His conversation was vague and unhelpful : his only coherent information that he wanted to see the " body in the bag " which was in the water.

Here was a serious matter requiring urgent investigation. So we escorted the prisoner to the phone box and detained him there while the police were summoned.

Bombing squads receiving training under Captain R. J. Harris in Victoria Park.

The police, too, took a serious view of the situation. They questioned the prisoner, decided that they also had better see the " body in the bag," and, not to be outdone, the night-patrol " went along."

Sure enough, there in the surf at the water's edge, lay a bag of a sort resembling a shroud.

Filled with a sense of our own importance we dragged the object to the sand, and, in the eerie darkness, we braced ourselves for the unpleasant task ahead—and cut the bag open.

There we stood gaping, peering closely. . . .

Not only one body did we find, but *three*. They were carcases of mutton washed up from a wreck. The night guard heaved a sigh and continued their patrols.

C.B.S.

THINGS WE WANT TO KNOW . . . .

1. Who was the Corporal who when on route march carried revolver, bayonet and binoculars ?

2. Who was the Sergeant who, investigating a blackout indiscretion, rang a front-door bell and was greeted immediately by a bright young thing in the smartest of dressing gowns who, gazing unseeingly into the darkness, excitedly declared, " Oh, do come in ; you've kept me waiting far too long " ?

3. Who arrived for duty with a suit of silk pyjamas, and whose mother brought down an extra pair of socks one stormy night ?

4. Who was the officer who during an early " Alert " ordered our sole rifle to be loaded " as we may be in action soon " ?

5. Who was the Sergeant who, challenging an R.A.F. Corporal and his lady friend in a shelter at 1 a.m., was surprised to hear the lady's reply : " You've come at rather an inconvenient moment, sergeant " ?

6. Who was the Invasion Committee member who was captured by " German paratroops " in Marldon Church stoke-hole on a Sunday morning ?

7. Who was the L.D.V. (later a Home Guard sergeant) who awakened late, dressed hastily and rushed on his son's cycle to Collaton road block—only to find he had mistaken the date ?

8. Who were the patrol who found a Marine Parade house a blaze of light and a notice on the front door : " Daddy, darling, we're not coming home tonight " ? The time was 12-30 a.m. Daddy must have been having a night out, too !

" HOOKY "

CHAPTER 12

"D" Company would have acquitted themselves valiantly, had they been put to the test, says a former O.C.

L.D.V. enthusiasm typified

BRIXHAM'S ZEAL

FROM the earliest days until the order to stand down the Brixham unit evinced a real enthusiasm which was reflected in the company's fine achievements. Unfortunately the Editor cannot recount them in detail for despite appeals for information few have seen fit to provide it ; indeed, but for the efforts of a former O.C., Lt.-Col. W. L. Parsons, who committed to paper details of the company's early history, Brixham would be very poorly represented in this book. This is a pity, for without a doubt Torquay and Paignton will desire to acknowledge the grand work of " D " Company during the war years and will be disappointed to find that the Editor has been barely able to do it justice.

However, since the greatest interest is probably to be found in the tale of Brixham's early organisation, " D " Company personnel may value the following recollections of Lt.-Col. Parsons even more than an account of their later activities, which are more firmly fixed in their memories.

Brixham has ever been zealous in a good cause and there was no lack of response to the appeal by Mr. Anthony Eden on May 15th, 1940. Brixham was subsequently responsible for four sections, Nos. 13, 14, 15 and 16, under the command of Capt. Hay Matthey ; Section 13 was drawn mostly from Higher Brixham, Section 14 from Lower Brixham, Section 15 from Kingswear and Section 16 from Churston Ferrers and Galmpton. By May 25th, the company's first emergency stand-to, 139 volunteers had enrolled.

Here are some of the names of those who made the formation of the Brixham unit possible :

Anderson F. N., Andrews J., Ansell A., Ash A. G., Baker J., Blackler W. H., Blenkin T. S., Bovey A. C., Bowers L. F., Bradden, E., Brazier A. H., Buckler, Buley P., Churchill J., Churchill J. S., Clarke, F. H., Clayton L. K., Clift G., Coates T. H., Coombes R. F., Coombes J. H., Coope S. H., Corde W. H., Cornish F., Crocker B. C.

Davey A. F., Davey D. C. E., Davies J. R. M., Davies R. D., Davis H., Dearson A. P., Dearson E. T., Desmond J. T., Dexter A.,

CAPT. HAY MATTHEY
Brixham's first O.C.

Dodd C. B., Dodd C. D., Dyer G. H., Earnsby A. E., Edmundson R. E., Evans H., Evans H., Foulger C. A., Fowler R. G., Fox E. F., Freer H. A. Galloway W. C. G., Giles F. A., Giles R. F. A., Glanville F. B., Glenn R. W., Harvey G. H., Harwood A. W., Hawkins J., Hawkins H. J., Hay G. B., Haywood G. D., Heath R. H., Hennion P. G. W., Hollows W. E., Hopkins G., Husson J. R., James P. S., Jarvis G. I., Jones F. W. D., Kingscote E. T., Knight E. G., Kyffin J. T., Keefe F., Lane W., Lawley G. H., Lee M., Lee S. W., Lidstone N. J., Lister E., Lovett Cameron, Luckham F., Luxton W. J., Mardon E. J., Marshall K., Matthey H. W., Martin A. H., Martin L. E., Martin J., Matthews S. W. E., Mills S. S., Mogridge J. D., Montgomery R. E. Neal R. S., Nicholl C. E., Norval A. F., Palmer E. C., Parker J. T., Parnell H. H., Parnell S. H., Parsons W. L., Partridge P. G., Percy W., Prattley G. W., Rickard A., Rockey F. T., Rump L. A., Sarah A. J. K., Sherriff H., Sherwin C., Shipley F., Shrives W. E., Shrives W. H., Silman W. T., Simpson F. R. B., Smardon W. R., Smith J. B., Snelson J. T., Stanbridge G. E., Stevens J., Symons H. H. Talbot E., Tamlin F. A., Taylor S. G., Thatcher S. H., Thomas C. R., Tolcher R. H., Treeby J. F., Tremlett C., Underwood W. F., Vincent S. J., Wade W., Wakeham R. F., Watson S. H., Williams B. G., Williams F. H., Williams S. F., Wills E. P., Woolston F. S., Worth G.

In order that there should be no misapprehension, we repeat that these are only some of the names.

Many others played memorable parts in those early and difficult days. A large proportion of them were past the prime of life and though still active and willing could hardly be expected to do long periods of service in all weathers and under all sorts of conditions. But that, in fact, is what they did and there must have been extremely few cases in which duty was neglected on account of age.

At Brixham's first emergency parade there were only six double-barrelled sporting guns (two 12 bores and four 16 bores), .22 sporting rifles and one old Lee-Enfield .303, these firearms being augmented by 12 leaden truncheons !

Neither staff nor accommodation having been provided, Capt. Hay Matthey had to scout around and find both. He succeeded. He took over the cottage adjoining the Brewery in Fore Street and made this H.Q. and was fortunate in obtaining the help of a lady, whose tact and pleasant manner, to say nothing of her efficiency in straightening out the office routine, made the life of L.D.Vs. in those hectic times a good deal more bearable than it might have been.

With coast watching forming the main part of the unit's duties, a post was at first established at Black Barn in Southdown Hill (Section 14) and later another one at Hill Head (Section 13) and though the numbers of men available were small, they were manned continuously by volunteers who did not quibble at double duty.

The job of Section 15 was to man a post near the railway at Kingswear and here, too, the former O.Cs. have spoken highly of the spirit of the men concerned.

On the completion of the Berry Head oil tanks the Black Barn post was ordered to be abandoned and a new post sited near them. After some trouble a disused cowshed was found at Ranscombe —it was in a terrible state but hard work and lime washing made it barely passable. It was a dreary place but Section 14 stuck it until another move was foreshadowed by the announcement that a new site would have to be found nearer Berry Head. This, it transpired, was at Louville Camp—a great improvement on the cowshed !

LT.-COL. W. L. PARSONS
Took over command of what later became " D " Company

Section 16 originally met at the Churston Golf House, then at the back of the Churston Railway Hotel, but accommodation was later found for them in the caretaker's room at the lavatories on Galmpton Warboro. Not an enticing address !

It was about August 1940 that Lt.-Col. Parsons took over command of the Brixham Company from Capt. Hay Matthey, the company at that time being charged with the defence of the 12 miles of coastline from Broadsands to the Brixham boundary at Kingswear.

Nothing was lacking in those days in the way of advice.

First the O.C. Company was told to have trenches dug at Mansands, with sandbag parapets. L.D.V. personnel were scarce but with the assistance of some of the more ardent volunteers and a great number of schoolboys, trenches were dug, by which time, of course, another Regular officer had arrived to proclaim them wrongly sited !

By the end of 1944 the Home Guard were familiar with this technique. Brixham's experience was not worse than other companies ; indeed it may have been a good deal happier. But there is no gainsaying the fact that a tremendous number of man-hours was wasted either because high ranking officers could not make up their minds or because when they did make them up they came to the wrong conclusions. It happened at Mansands. Trenches were again partly dug in new positions but before completion there was another change of direction and men were told to embark on trenches at Hill Head to protect the road block there.

It was said at the time—and has certainly been said many times since—that the road block was practically useless and it says something for the morale of the Brixham unit—and for that matter the

MAJOR PUGHE-MORGAN, T.D.
Lt.-Col. Parson's successor

entire Home Guard—that they refused to be depressed, though their comments are best forgotten !

However, the trenches were dug and the sandbags filled and with the news that a highly placed officer was coming to inspect this example of Brixham's energetic output, men worked to complete them within 48 hours by sticking to the task on Saturday afternoon and Sunday. No-one will be surprised to learn that the officer concerned did not in fact inspect them. That was something that experience taught us to expect.

But to return to Hill Head. The next news was that a flame thrower was to be provided. So more trenches were dug to house the flame thrower and bombing crews.

And then Brixham was told that Mansands and Hill Head were to be abandoned and a new defence line nearer the town was to be decided.

Weeks of argument concerning the siting of the new defence line followed, and of that troublesome period Lt.-Col. Parsons has written :

" I well remember meeting a Major General to show him Hill Head and Mansands. He arrived at Hill Head and then went to Southdown, but when he saw the road down to Mansands and knew he would have to walk there and back he jibbed and instead asked to be taken to a spot where he could obtain a bird's eye view of Brixham. He was conducted to Black Barn, and turning to the Brigadier said with a lordly wave of his arm, ' There is your defence line.' When the intervening valleys and hills were pointed out to him he merely told the Brigadier to settle the problem himself.

" The new defence line (a useless one, in my view) commenced at Northern Hills, running across the cricket field, and thence across Furzeham Common to Battery Road. And with a total strength of 170 men we had to defend 12 miles of coast line, immobilise petrol pumps, defend road blocks and man the Perimeter Defence ! "

The Company did, of course, have its lighter moments and a great many friendships formed "on parade" have proved to be worth preserving.

Early members may yet recall having assisted the police to round-up a supposed spy who was believed to have taken photographs at Scabbacombe. The squad searched from Kingston Farm to the sea. The police searched with equal diligence from Boohay to the sea. And the " spy " was caught—a member of a neighbouring Home Guard Company, who was on a natural history expedition—

and, so the story goes, ran when challenged because he thought he was trespassing.

There is, too, the tale of the platoon which became lost in the darkness at Scabbacombe and of the coast watchers on the same beach who, seeing what they believed to be lights, challenged, and, receiving no reply, expended their ammunition on what was afterwards thought to have been phosphorus-laden waves !

Lt.-Col. Parsons, proud of his own association with this volunteer force, has concluded his notes with the following passage :

" I would like to thank again all officers and men of " D " Company for the support given me while I had the honour of commanding it.

" Broadly speaking, for the first eighteen months everything—with the exception of military supplies—was done voluntarily and I take off my hat to the L.D.V. and those civilians who helped to make and maintain such a force in their midst. I thank God that, with their lack of weapons, they were never put to the test, but I am confident that if they had been "D" Company would have acquitted themselves valiantly."

Subsequently the Company, under Major R. B. Pughe-Morgan, T.D., who succeeded Lt.-Col. Parsons in command, went from strength to strength with the arrival of arms, which were supplied on a scale which could at last be regarded as commensurate with the importance of the Brixham unit.

For all-round proficiency " D " Company would have been

Waiting for the word "Dismiss." " D " Company on parade.

hard to beat and few had a more responsible task.

Lieut. Maurice E. Behar, Battalion Signal Officer, and one time member of the Churston Platoon, has written of the enthusiasm with which training was undertaken, adding :

" No opportunity was lost where advantage could be taken of the presence of Service units to carry out exercises and mock battles. The experience gained and knowledge learned at each was carefully recorded on battle boards and a ' post-mortem ' was always held, so that each member was able to gain a fine and unique knowledge of the strategic value of the country which he was to defend.

" It has always been a matter of amazement how men who were tired and harassed by an excess of wartime work returned home in the evening and, with barely time to have a meal and change into their uniform, were on parade for drill, lectures or exercises with almost scrupulous regularity.

" The generous spirit and happy co-operation coupled with a fine enthusiasm, were the qualities that enabled the Brixham Company to reach the high standard that was achieved."

With which view Torquay and Paignton are doubtless in the fullest accord.

The Colonel inspecting " D " Company's Guard of Honour in September, 1943.

CHAPTER 13

No Company did more important—or more varied—work than "H," as this chapter will surely show.

The Gas Company's distinction—

H.G.s DESTROY F.W. 190

"H" COMPANY mainly comprised the staffs of undertakings which volunteered to protect the public services on which both civilian and military personnel were so dependent. They formed an integral, and highly important, part of the battalion organisation and it is to their activities that this chapter is devoted.

The one exception to the general rule of the company was the No. I Platoon. This had no connection with any of the Public Utility undertakings, but sprang from the Torquay Platoon of the South Devon Mobile Company and concluded its chequered existence as the Gunner Platoon at Corbyn's Head.

Older members will remember the early efforts to form a mobile striking force and of the popular appeal this unit had for the younger and more active men. Their training was obtained under the direction of the 2nd Gloucester Regiment, and if only half the stories one heard at the time were true, this was strenuous indeed, entailing some remarkably full-blooded exercises on Dartmoor, one of the most memorable of which was an attack from Lustleigh village to Manaton across Lustleigh Cleave in the middle of a snow storm. There is, of course, nothing unique in war-time of young men crawling in the snow. What is surprising at this distant date, however, is that they should *volunteer* for it.

The platoon's first O.C. was Mr. F. A. Larkworthy, and its second, Lieut. J. H. Chapple, but with the call-up of younger men in July, 1941, the Mobile Company was disbanded and its Torquay members transferred to the Torbay Battalion as 23 Platoon. Lieut. Snelson took over from Lieut. Chapple in the same year and at that time half the platoon was used to augment the battery of Regulars at Corbyn's Head, the other half to defend the approaches to the battery. Subsequently Capt. H. Grant, who had previously been the Battalion Gas Instructor and then the officer in charge of the defences from the Spa Ballroom to Corbyn's Head, succeeded Lieut. Snelson, with Lieut. Peters as second-in-command, and the whole personnel

CAPT. H. GRANT
O.C. HI. *Platoon (Gunners)*

became gunners. Interest in training was of so high a standard that a number of the personnel spent their holidays with the battery to gain further knowledge in gunnery, and several others spent a week at the Citadel, Plymouth, and all had excellent reports at the subsequent examination.

The battery in its early days consisted of a number of gunners, Royal Artillery, augmented by the Home Guard, but it eventually resolved itself into a battery composed entirely of Home Guards with just a few of the Regulars attached for maintenance.

A high standard was essential in this platoon, for not only had infantry training to be taught, but also gunnery, searchlights, engines, Barr and Stroud range-finder, Bofors and Rocket guns, Spigot Mortar, 75 mm. guns, 6-pdr. guns, Bren guns and aircraft identification.

The platoon's strength was maintained at between 80 and 100 and the average attendance on parade was always somewhere in the region of 90 per cent. and the platoon's record was one of which every man could be proud, were he a member of the first mobile unit in 1940 or one of the efficient gunners of 1944.

★ ★ ★

Nos. 2 and 3 Platoons (Torquay and Paignton Gas Company) originated as 17a and 17b Sections of "F" Company (Torquay Division) Local Defence Volunteers, and from the date of their formation until September 10th, 1944, maintained an unbroken record of nightly guards, and patrols, as an integral part of Torbay's coastal defence.

For the first month or two patrols were armed with a solitary shot-gun of private ownership and pick shafts loaded with lead at the base. One service rifle did come into the possession of the unit, but in a few days was withdrawn and substituted by two French carbines of doubtful fighting value.

The unit, now numbering 160 strong, was responsible for the defence of the Hollacombe Gas Manufacturing Station and railway sidings of the Torquay and Paignton Gas Company, which are actually situated above a beach suitable for landing craft. The unit carried out its own defence works, which included several strongly constructed pill-boxes, not only commanding the beach approaches but around the perimeter of the works so as to make a strong point or "island of resistance."

The fire-power of the unit in the later days was provided by rifles, Stens, L.M.Gs., B.M.Gs., Northover Projectors, Boyes A/Tk. rifles, E.Y. rifles and grenades. In addition the unit erected and manned a "Z" A/A battery, consisting of a U.P. (unrotating projectile) radiator or rocket projector. The anti-aircraft role of the unit took a place of prominence in its structure, in view of the vulnerable and military nature of the works and plant, which could rightly be regarded as a legitimate target for hostile aircraft.

From the railway embankment, which provides an uninterrupted view of Torbay, patrols kept ceaseless observation from dusk to dawn for four and a half years without a break. Every guard was paraded and inspected, without exception, by the Orderly Officer for the day in true ceremonial manner before dusk. The maintenance of these guards and patrols, having regard to the long hours and difficult black-out working conditions imposed by war-time restrictions on a gas undertaking, was no mean achievement. A considerable number of the members worked an average of seven shifts per week, while day workers averaged some 60 hours per week. In addition to the Home Guard duties, every officer and N.C.O. in the two platoons performed full A.R.P. duties and "stood to" on the 700-odd alerts in the Torbay area and attended to broken gas mains and services and other bombed premises as required. The long hours of watching through the winter nights were not always quiet. If the patrol were not fighting their way in the howling winds along the exposed sea frontage they were straining in the stillness and darkness for signs of enemy activity.

A note in the handwriting of the Orderly Officer for the day takes memory back to the black days of September, 1940, when the Home Guard, inadequately equipped and armed, stood by to repel the expected invader.

"1245 hours Sunday, September 8th, 1940. Message received from Battalion Headquarters—Port Commander has manned all his posts 100 per cent—will we do the same. Be prepared to stand-to during the night with gas masks.

With the Gunners at Corbyn's Head.

CAPT. R. C. TAYLOR, M.B.E., M.M.
O.C. H2. and H3. Platoons (Torquay and Paignton Gas Company)

State of emergency has arisen."

At 0930 hours on the next day, September 9th, 1940, the tension was relieved by the message notifying that the situation was back to normal, and extra men could be recalled.

The following letter from O.C. H. Company is worth recording as a reminder of those days when every movement was suspect and vigilance of first importance :

" I have to acknowledge your letter of the 28th July, 1941, reporting the incident on the 25th instant, when the guard on your Observation Post was compelled to open fire on a boat which ignored challenge.

" I have spoken to R.N.O. about the incident and he has agreed that in future notice of the movement of these patrol boats should be given in advance. He has undertaken to do this.

" Lt.-Col. Sloggett has asked me to say that he wishes to congratulate your men not only on their vigilance but on their markmanship—one shot at least passing between two of the occupants and entering the side of the boat—too close to be comfortable it is considered ! To avoid such incidents in future, action as stated above will be taken by the Naval Authority."

Again on the night of Monday, March 14th, 1942, the stillness was broken by the splashing of oars in the water and the " stand-to " signal was sent down to the guard room.

As the guard took up stations a shot was fired by the N.C.O. on patrol who had observed a light some 200 yards out to sea, and the guard were not without some misgivings as they mounted their machine gun.

As no answering signals were given to the signal letter which was flashed out, a dark object was engaged with short bursts, and later the beach was searched. The remains of a rubber dinghy were found but no further explanation of the " incident of the light " was obtained.

Of a more serious nature was an incident which occurred during the evening of Friday, September 4th, 1942, when the Gas Works suffered damage by enemy action and a $1\frac{1}{2}$ million cubic feet gas holder was set ablaze by cannon and machine gun fire. Home Guards of H2/3. Platoons figured conspicuously in the work of mastering the fire, which threatened with the fall of darkness to act as an excellent target indicator to other enemy aircraft operating at that time against a convoy of shipping passing up the Channel. The following were highly commended for their work on this occasion and received letters of commendation and congratulation from Lt.-Gen. H. C. Lloyd, G.O.C. Southern Command :—

Capt. R. C. Taylor
Pte. E. Chard
Lieut. J. W. Denton
Sgt. F. Richardson
Pte. H. Windeatt
Sergt. F. C. Williams
Sergt. J. Vanstone
Captain C. H. Fursdon

At subsequent investitures held by His Majesty the King, Capt. R. C. Taylor received the honour of the M.B.E., and Lieut. J. W. Denton and Sergt. F. C. Richardson were recipients of the George Medal.

LIEUT. J. W. DENTON, G.M.

The enemy continued his activity against targets in the area by a number of tip-and-run raids and it became necessary to man continuously the Lewis guns and the " Z " type radiator. The long hours of watching and waiting were soon to be rewarded—for to the Gas Company went the distinction of destroying a Hun.

The following report established this claim to having destroyed an enemy hit-and-run raider, a F.W. 190, during the morning of December 30th, 1942 :—

" At approximately 1012 hours on December 30th, 1942, three planes approached Hollacombe Gas Works from landward.

" Two planes identified as F.W. 190s approached over Round Hill flying east at approximately 400 feet. The third plane, identified as a F.W. 190, approached via Cockington Valley over No. 1 Holder at approximately 150 feet with its machine guns in action, but apparently with no effect.

" Sergt. W. P. Matthews, in charge as No. 1 on U.P. Projector, identified and engaged the two planes flying over Round Hill and approaching the projector position at an angle of 90º to the port side.

" Ten rounds were immediately discharged at the leading plane. These rounds were extremely well directed and caused the plane to kick violently in the air whilst small sections of material were observed to fall into the sea below. The plane immediately dived towards the sea apparently out of control, but recovered almost on water level and proceeded towards Berry Head at a much reduced speed.

" It would appear highly improbable that the plane would reach its home base for it was apparently losing speed and unable later to rejoin formation with its flight. I understand from outside witnesses of the incident that a plane was seen to crash in the sea off Berry Head, but we are unable to say if this is the plane hit by the U.P. discharged by Sergt. Matthews. Our attention was directed at this stage to recharging the projector for further action.

" The second plane was engaged with the second bank of rocket projectiles, but the shots were not close. This plane con-

SGT. F. C. RICHARDSON, G.M.

tinued in an easterly direction, being joined by the third plane mentioned.

"Lieut. J. W. Denton, who was present, and Pte. F. Powell, who was No. 2 on the gun, confirmed the above.

"In all 18 rockets were discharged, one remaining in projector and one falling short on the beach and not detonating.

"The discharged rocket projectile was pulled out of the sand on the morning of December 31st, 1942, and is now attached by cord to a stake. The matter has been reported to the R.N.O., Torquay, and to the Police, Torquay."

The unit very proudly painted a swastika on the gun when the following signal was received from Col. H. G. Hay, Commanding South Devon Group Home Guard :

"The Devon Sub District Commander has read with pleasure the report by the Gas Works Company of the Torbay Battalion of their action with enemy aircraft on December 30th, 1942.

"Although no confirmation can be obtained, it is a fact that one F.W. 190 did crash into the sea off Berry Head on the morning of December 30th. I think it can be assumed that this machine was the one hit by Sgt. Matthews.

"Please convey to Capt. Taylor and all ranks under his command, the Sub District Commander's appreciation of the work carried out.

"It is suggested that a board be placed in the Company H.Q. with record of this and any future machines brought to earth.

"The Zone Commander and I are very pleased to be able to forward these remarks and wish to add our appreciation to that of the Sub District Commander."

Platoon parades were regularly held and attendances were very satisfactory. Frequent exercises were organised to test the strength of the defences from all angles, and these were entered into by the members of the unit with very great keenness and rivalry. The platoons also took part with enthusiasm in the exercises and training parades held under battalion arrangements, and had reason to be proud of some of its activities, in particular the capture from the "enemy" of three Bren gun carriers operating against the battalion.

It is pleasing to place on record the following general remarks from an Inspecting Officer's Report, following the critical inspection of the platoons at action stations for the Battalion Manning Exercise held on Sunday, March 26th, 1944 :—

"A thoroughly well organised and efficient locality. The administration arrangements are well organised and all ranks

are fully in the picture."
In notifying the Inspecting Officer's Report it was particularly gratifying to receive the following letter from Lt.-Col. A. J. H. Sloggett, D.S.O. :—
"In sending you the attached report by the Devon Sub District Inspecting Officer, I would like to congratulate all ranks in your platoon on the excellent results obtained. There is no doubt that the general remarks made by the Inspecting Officer are thoroughly deserved."
The total strength at the date of "stand down" on November 1st, 1944, was 5 Officers and 140 Other Ranks.

LIEUT. L. W. OLIVER
Succeeded Lieut. G. J. Hollyer as O.C. H4. Platoon (Torquay Electricity Undertaking)

★ ★ ★

The Electricity Commissioners having endorsed the Government's appeal and pointed out that the duty of volunteers would be to defend the property of their own undertaking, 88 men employed by the Torquay Electricity Undertaking enrolled and became Section 18 of "F" (Torquay) Company, with G. J. Hollyer and L. W. Oliver as joint section leaders.

Dusk till dawn guard duties were commenced on June 24th, 1940, at the undertaking's three most important Torquay sub-stations, namely :—

        No. 1—Lawes Bridge.
        No. 2—Upton Valley.
        No. 3—St. Marychurch.

Intercommunication was possible through the undertaking's supervisory telephone system and regular reports, including air raid warnings, were transmitted to and from the operator in the central control room. These reports were recorded in duplicate and subsequently checked by the section leaders.

Although several other V.Ps. on the undertaking warranted consideration, it was agreed that with the strength available, full protection could not be given to more than these three sub-stations, although the Lymington Road depot and Electric House were to be covered in the event of "action stations."

The section had no arms or ammunition when these duties were commenced and the most useful weapons conceivable were pick shafts with the heads drilled out to receive a couple of pounds of molten lead. Even after rifles were issued, many of the older and non-military minded members preferred to carry a loaded pick shaft rather than a firearm during their night's vigil !

One of these men, 60 years of age, was heard one night to challenge in his Welsh dialect thus—" I am afraid I must ask you to stop." Another would consistently challenge—" Halt, who comes here ? "

By July 1st, 1940, the strength of the section had risen to 94, but almost immediately resignations due to the call-up began to come in. Seven rifles and 70 rounds were issued to the section early in this month, enabling sentries to carry five rounds. At the end of the month rifles on charge numbered 20 with 400 rounds, and some musketry instruction was possible.

At the end of August, the first denims and steel helmets were received. By September the first battle dresses and boots had been issued, but it was not until March, 1941, that all ranks were more or less fully kitted, with the exception of a few outsize battle dresses and respirators.

From October 1st, 1940, Section 18 became No. 18 Platoon with G. J. Hollyer as O.C., and L. W. Oliver as second-in-command. At the end of this year, due to the continued call-up of men, the platoon strength was down to 82, all ranks.

In January, 1941, serious regular parades and instructions commenced with Sgt. W. F. Hallion and Cpl. F. B. Cowling as instructors, and the platoon, in addition to carrying out its nightly guard duties, managed to send three men per night for four weeks to the assistance of the undertaking's Newton Abbot platoon (of the 9th Battalion), to augment their guard on the Power Station. It was also decided at this time to appoint two motor cycle despatch riders for use in emergency intercommunications.

By the end of 1941 the platoon strength was 68, i.e., 2 officers (Lieut. G. J. Hollyer and Sec. Lieut. L. W. Oliver) and 66 other ranks. Fourteen volunteers were lost to the platoon through resignations as a result of the compulsory training regulations. The strength in March, 1942, was 53 (2 officers, 51 other ranks).

G.W.R. Platoon personnel with their anti-aircraft gun.

A special beach lighting section, comprising three N.C.Os. and nine men was formed in March, 1942, their particular function at " action stations " being to stand by the controls of the lighting installed on Torquay beaches.

In May, 1942, the Platoon Commander, Lieut. G. J. Hollyer, was compelled to resign for business reasons, and the second-in-command, Sec. Lieut. L. W. Oliver, was promoted to Lieutenant to succeed him. Sgt. W. F. Hallion was subsequently appointed to Sec. Lieut. and to be second-in-command. Platoon strength at the end of 1942 was 49 (2 officers, 47 other ranks).

In January, 1943, No. 18 Platoon became H4. and during this year only three men were lost to the platoon, one of these due unfortunately to the death of L/Cpl. H. Harvey, a very popular N.C.O., and at the end of 1943 platoon strength was 44 (2 officers, 42 other ranks), at which it remained until duties terminated.

No. 5 Platoon of " H " Company was the Great Western Railway, which was subsequently transferred to " A " Company.

LIEUT. H. S. LEWIS
O.C. H5. Platoon, subsequently A5. Platoon (G.W.R.)

No. 6 Platoon (Devon General Omnibus Company) was originally 22 Platoon and concluded its career as a company of the Devon and Cornwall Transport Column.

But to go back to the beginning, early in June, 1940, a number of the Head Office clerical and engineering employees of the Omnibus Company attended the training and instructional courses being given to members of the newly formed L.D.V. It was not at first clear whether public services would have to be maintained in an emergency or whether the whole organisation might be moved to another district, and training therefore proceeded for some weeks before enrolment forms were signed.

This uncertainty was soon settled and in the latter days of June, 1940, a unit was formed based on the Omnibus Depot and Works at Newton Road, Torquay, this commencing with two leaders and 41 other ranks, who were given the task of protecting the omnibus buildings and fleet and were in the nature of a factory unit.

A competent instructor was found, training and drilling were regularised and a guard was mounted on the buildings during evenings, nights and at week-ends. A guard room, sleeping equipment and other facilities came along in due course.

Strong points and defensive positions were constructed and patrols soon learned the local topography even down to molehills !

At the end of 1940 the strength was 2 officers with 79 other ranks.

In the early days of 1941, orders were received to enrol and to train omnibus drivers in Home Guard duties to man civilian buses earmarked for use by the Army in case of need. The factory unit, now known as Platoon 22 of the Torbay Battalion, therefore enrolled some 50 drivers.

To ensure the maintenance of essential works and civilian services the vehicles earmarked were to be drawn from other towns as well as Torquay and so it came about that units comprising vehicles and Home Guard drivers were formed at Torquay, Kingsteignton, Exeter, Exmouth and Sidmouth,

MAJOR R. G. JAMES
O.C. D.G. Platoons, which later became a company of the Devon and Cornwall Transport Column

During 1941 No. 22 Platoon continued training with a gradually increasing armament and growing proficiency.

On one occasion a very young member of the company on guard duty was displaying to a group of admirers his recently acquired skill in loading and unloading his rifle and both the demonstrator and his friends suffered considerable shock when on the final " pulling-off " a live round which had remained in the breech was fired. Fortunately no-one suffered any hurt but the incident greatly increased the vigilance with which non-Home Guards approached the premises after dark !

In the late summer of 1941 instructions were received to discontinue factory guard duties and later in the year No. 22 Platoon was included in the defence system of the town itself, being assigned to defensive positions covering an important road block on a main road.

As defenders of this road block and of the neighbouring omnibus workshops No. 22 Platoon invariably took a prominent and not unworthy part in the exercise attacks on Torquay.

In January, 1942, a separate unit, to be named Platoon No. 19, was formed from the ranks of No. 22 with 2 officers and 68 of the drivers then attached to No. 22. The strength of Platoon 22 after the transfer was also 2 officers and 68 other ranks. While close and happy co-operation was maintained, Platoons 22 and 19 now had separate roles and suitable separate training. No. 22 continued its general service character while No. 19 undertook R.A.S.C. training. The wide geographical "spread" of sub-units in No. 19 made centralised training impossible but in each sub-unit the right man or men took up the tasks of learning and passing-on instructional matter provided by R.A.S.C. in lectures, demonstrations and in literature.

In March, 1942, Platoon 22 was given coastal patrol duties and carried out these duties for a long period.

In November the designation "Platoon 22" was changed to "Platoon H6."

Throughout 1942 Platoon 19 worked hard at training and exercising, at the end of the year attaining a strength of 2 officers and 92 other ranks, and in November its title became Platoon 1, "G" Coach Company Devon Home Guard.

January 1943 was another milestone and saw the unit changed to 2135 Motor Coach Company, but still attached to its parent Torbay Battalion. Its amended and greatly increased establishment of vehicles, equipment and personnel brought to the unit increased work and responsibilities.

In March, 1943, 10th Battalion approved the transfer of part of Platoon H6. to 2135 Company and in May the transfer of the second part of H6. was approved. The strength of the company became 7 officers and some 210 other ranks, and in November, 1944, the strength was 8 officers and 196 other ranks.

February, 1944, saw the formation of the Devon and Cornwall Transport Column Home Guard with headquarters in Exeter and 2135 Company became a constituent company of the Column.

No. 2135 Company parted with regret from the 10th Torbay Battalion, whose "directions, wise guidance and ever-ready practical help had made the birth and upbringing of the company possible," states their O.C., Major R. G. James.

With the majority of its personnel working their civilian duties in shifts and on Saturday afternoons and Sundays, attendance records could never be good. The onerous work of checking and watching attendance records had its lighter moments. On one occasion a regular attender was absent without leave from a Sunday morning parade. He explained that after finishing work at mid-day on Saturday he was suddenly taken ill and did not recover until Sunday night. To clear his reputation and as solid proof of his statement he went on to explain that he was so unwell that he couldn't even play football on Saturday afternoon !

In the Autumn of 1940 Lieut. P. T. Read was appointed to form a Communications Section covering B.H.Q. and all companies, and while many new members joined for this purpose, it was then permissible to utilise the services of car-owners who were not able or desirous of enrolling as L.D.Vs. The section soon totalled upwards of fifty in the Battalion area and in the early days functioned in all exercises, both in transport of troops and message

A Devon General unit erects a Newton Road road-block.

carrying. The L.D.V. members had no arms at that time but large wrenches and tyre levers were always on hand ! In 1942 it became known as the Transport Section, and car drivers not enrolled were dispensed with. The method adopted by higher-ups left a lot to be desired ; there were no thanks for services rendered, no explanations, just an intimation that these people should no longer be used. However, one lady continued to assist " B " Company, a Miss Matthews of St. Marychurch, who turned out at five and six o'clock every morning to bring home the patrols from Walls Hill and Marine Drive.

Motor cycles became an " issue " later and message carrying improved so much that in a 24-hour exercise the Regulars laid a trap to catch one D.R., a Pte. Bird. They kept him a prisoner at their headquarters at the Clarence Hotel, but his report said he " knew nuffink," survived their torture and enjoyed their rations !

★ ★ ★

In January of 1941 companies were asked to submit names of volunteers for Signals—Morse and Semaphore. Among the names submitted was A. W. Strike of " C " Company, who was promoted to Lieut., and appointed Signals Officer. Subsequently he was succeeded by Lieut. M. E. Behar. Sgt. R. J. Stevens was appointed Signal Sergeant for Torquay ; Sgt. R. P. Finch for Paignton and Sgt. H. G. MacDonald for Brixham ; Cpl. Warren " A " Company ; Cpl. Leaman, " B " Company ; Cpl. Coath, " C " Company ; L/Cpl. E. V. Jordain, " D " Company ; Cpl. J. V. T. Warn, " F " Company ; L/Cpl. Jennings, " H " Company ; and Sgt. W. G. Hexter was sergeant in charge of wireless communications with Cpl. S. A. Cooper to assist. Mrs. M. Edmunds was appointed in charge of the Women's Auxiliary Home Guard Signallers.

It has been said that signallers should be chosen from the " cream " of a unit. In order to qualify for the classification of Home Guard signalman, a high standard of intelligence, enthusiasm and courage was essential. It can truly be said that each signalman in this unit possessed an abundance of each of these qualities. As soon as the necessity and importance of communications was realised, the section got to work—field line communications between companies was considered necessary—visual signals with lamp and flag could not be overlooked—despatch riders, pigeons, P.O. telephones, signal offices and terminals all had to be installed and equipped.

The provision of equipment was a formidable barrier and no other voluntary service has ever begged, borrowed, stolen or improvised more effectively than the 10th (Torbay) Signal Section !

Suffice to say that when " D " Day came, every conceivable means of communication was available : between 20-30 miles of field cable had been laid and maintained, teams of wireless operators had been trained, and the section earned high praise for its standard of wireless procedure and security.

At this time the services of the Home Guard Women Auxiliaries had been enlisted, and a high proportion of the many laurels earned by the section was due to the keen and efficient enthusiasm of these girls. In the early days Signals were looked upon as a comic people apart, who hatched plots in basements and could occasionally be seen from afar waving flags or flashing lamps—an impression that soon gave way to feelings of respect. Company commanders and platoon commanders, as well as those in command of mobile striking forces, came to appreciate the many advantages of an efficient wireless set in the field, and the usefulness of trained signallers capable of establishing and maintaining communications wherever and whenever they were needed.

CAPT. P. T. READ, M.B.E, M.M.
Intelligence Officer and Assistant Adjutant. Former Transport and Communications Officer

During the latter days of 1943, when the theatre of war was moving towards Western Europe, and the question of " Where and when will the Second Front open ? " was on all lips, training in the signal section had reached its zenith, and members had even attended courses at Catterick. It will always be a matter of wonder as to how these part-time civilian soldiers, harassed as they were with their own onerous war work, found it possible to devote the time and effort required to form a specialist unit which earned for itself a far-reaching reputation.

★   ★   ★

Pigeons, too, played their part in Battalion Communications. The official representative for the Army Pigeon supply was Mr. C. J. Donovan, of Chelston, who helped considerably, and the battalion expert was Cpl. Thompson, of " B " Company, who soon had available pigeons trained from all Company HQs. to surrounding towns. Pigeons were used on all exercises of the battalion and more than once took part in a Southern Command tie-up—Salisbury to Penzance.

One amusing incident is worth recording. It concerns an all-day exercise in which pigeons were to be used from companies to B.H.Q. It was not possible to reverse this service without training, but Major Pughe-Morgan, O.C. of " D " Company, asked if he could send over some local pigeons, which was agreed. The time arrived to use them, messages were affixed and the birds thrown up, but to the amusement of all one just flew around and came back to the feet of the sender with a delightful chuckle. The bird was pushed a little higher a second time, but with no better luck. It settled on the roof a second, came back to the feet of the sender and then decided to walk. And off it went towards the town and—no more was seen of it.

The " pigeon," it transpired, was a fantail !

LIEUT. M. E. BEHAR
Promoted from " D " Company
Intelligence to Bn. Signal Officer

When, in 1941, instructions were issued for a Battalion Intelligence Section to be formed and trained, it commenced its long course under the able instruction of Major Ball. Later, representatives of all companies attended and over a period of six months the whole section became fully conversant with this specialised job and knew every yard of the battalion area.

Following Major Ball's promotion to second-in-command of the battalion, Lieut. P. T. Read took over, and on Battalion H.Q. moving to Cambridge Lodge, the section was provided with a room for its own use and to accommodate the maps.

By 1943 the section was sufficiently trained to impart its story to the platoons, and a complete syallabus of intelligence lectures was given to all ranks by section personnel. By this time it had been organised down to companies. To " A " Company went Sgt. Callard (later Capt. Callard of R.E.M.E.), followed by Sgt. Martin, M.A. ; to " B " Company Sgt. Wilkinson (who was honoured in June 1944 with a Certificate of Merit) ; " C " and " F " Company were under Lieut. Durnell and " D " Company under Lieut. Behar, who, on leaving to become Signal Officer, was replaced by Lieut. Price.

In November, 1942, Capt. Read attended a camouflage course at the Army-Air Force Co-operation aerodrome at Salisbury and persuaded the O.C. (by what means we are not informed !) to send a plane to Exeter for purposes of military instruction.

In 1943 arrangements were completed and a party of 48 left on what proved to be the coldest day of the winter to take part in air reconnaisance. Eight trips were made over an area covering Dartmouth—Brixham, and the experience will be long remembered by Intelligence personnel not only on account of the extreme cold, which, according to an informant literally turned Major Bentley blue, but because of the outstanding achievement in getting the Authorities to send a plane and crew from Salisbury for our own especial benefit.

If only other departments had been as equally helpful !

No. 21 Platoon, which provided the Battalion H.Q. night guard, was recruited from the staff of the Prudential Assurance Company, which was evacuated from London to Torquay.

Commanded by Lieut. A. L. Coombes and Lieut. W. Marsh, some 70 members of the staff enlisted in the first week of the L.D.V., and in the early days the unit was responsible for the coastal area from Meadfoot to the Imperial Hotel. Battalion guard duties were carried on without a break until the Prudential returned to London in November, 1943, Lieut. Samson being left in charge of stores and the few remaining members.

It is as well to make clear that not all the Prudential employees were members of this platoon. The Editor has no figures to prove his contention but it is likely that as many belonged to other platoons as belonged to No. 21. It is an indisputable fact that practically every platoon commander in "A" and "B" Companies has had occasion to be grateful to a Prudential man, and it is safe to say that no organisation was subsequently so greatly missed.

With the company's departure for London, the fate of the remaining personnel was in the balance, but compulsory enrolments enabled the platoon to be brought up to strength and the duties at Battalion H.Q. were continued. Subsequently, however, the platoon was transferred to "B" Company, where, after training in the Intake Platoon at Audley Park, it was commanded by Lieut. G. H. Lidstone, with Sec. Lieut. M. W. Lowndes Pateman as second-in-command, Lieut. Samson having transferred to H.Q.

There is little that can be said for the unit following the introduction of compulsory enrolments, for the abnormally large proportion of conscripted personnel weighed heavily against all attempts to foster a spirit of comradeship and service. The loyal few (and fortunately there were some who could not have been bettered in the most enthusiastic unit) worked well. They included the N.C.Os. who had previously laboured as instructors in the Intake Platoon, and others who were largely self-trained, thanks to their own initiative and their desire for proficiency.

"OFFENDING OBJECT" ON THE GOLF COURSE

Members of the Home Guard were called upon to perform many queer tasks and not the least among them fell to the lot of the Permanent Staff.

There was, for instance. the case of one who, being called upon by the Torquay Golf Club to remove an object believed to be a bomb from the fairway of the course, discovered it to be nothing more dangerous than an unusually shaped electric torch !

But quite as good as any was the following which happened to the Adjutant. Let him relate the story himself :

" 'The Police on the phone for you, Sir.'

" Taking up the receiver I listened to the familiar voice of Sgt. Bolt of the Torquay Police. Would I, asked Sgt. Bolt, send the Battalion Gas Officer to the police station to identify a cylinder of gas which had been handed in ?

" Everyone handed in their ' finds ' to Sgt. Bolt and he usually called upon the Home Guard to help identify them, and, if dangerous, to remove and destroy them. " But this was a bit too much. A cylinder of gas! This must be attended to at once. "And so the Gas Officer was contacted and asked to take the matter in hand.

"I hoped that that ended the affair. Our Gas Officer was fully qualified to deal with such a thing and would no doubt report later on. "And sure enough he did.

"'Gas! That cylinder you sent me to see doesn't contain gas. It must be something explosive!' This over the phone from him. I thought his tone very pleasant considering he had left his work on a wild goose chase! He was a busy man.

"I muttered apologies and told him that I would get the Ammunition Officer to have a look at it. This was not so good. I must do something about it for Sgt. Bolt might blow himself up!

"The Ammunition Officer promised to look into it as soon as he could and once more I felt that the matter was in good hands.

"The next day a parcel arrived at Battalion H.Q. containing the offending object. No danger labels, no warning not to touch. Just a short note passing it on to me.

"I gingerly peeped at the contents. The cylinder had been divided into two parts. On the lid of one half I read

COCOA ESSENCE

and on the other

BEEF EXTRACT

"And on the side was stamped—1894."

Torquay as seen by the Intelligence Section on their reconnaissance flight

CHAPTER 14

As a tribute to those who died we print this account by Captain C. H. Fursdon, E.D., of the Corbyn's Head explosion.

Six lives were claimed in the

GUN SITE TRAGEDY

THE evening of August 11, 1944, was clear. A cool breeze whispered through the trees around the Corbyn's Head battery of coastal artillery. We were there to witness another practice shoot, as was the Brigadier Royal Artillery, Southern Command, and the Commander Coast Artillery, South West District.

The spectators gazed seaward. We were proud of this detachment attached to a Regular Coastal Artillery unit. They had earned praise for consistently good work and fine shooting, and we wished them luck.

The guns had fired and were ranging ; then a delay occurred on one of them. Orders and acknowledgments snapped out, we raised our binoculars in expectation.

Fire ! There was a muffled explosion.

The guns were firing at over three thousand yards, but the round had plunged into the sea one thousand yards away.

And looking towards the offending gun we observed a sheet of flame creeping outside the gun emplacement, devouring grass and camouflage, and though the situation had not dawned upon the majority, tragedy was being enacted before our eyes.

And then realisation came. The breech of the gun had blown and men had died. Others were seriously injured or badly burned. Only the very lucky ones escaped.

And with this knowledge things began to move. Our medical officer took charge of the lecture hut, which was turned into a dressing station, and in his quiet, efficient manner, proceeded to do his best for the injured. An ambulance was soon on the scene and other doctors came to our aid. The flames, too, were soon under control.

The casualties were hurried to the Torbay Hospital and a hush of horror descended upon those left behind. Four Home Guards had been killed instantaneously and one Regular artilleryman and another Home Guard later died of their injuries.

Then came the roll call and a few words of encouragement from the BRA. Men manned and fired another gun to break the spell, the assembly dismissed and we went our ways.

To Capt. Grant, the officer in command of the Home Guard detachment, accompanied by the Adjutant, fell the duty of breaking the sad news to the relatives of the casualties.

One cannot pass on without recording the deep sympathy and keen interest shown by the BRA and the CCA, the former visiting the families of the men and personally interesting himself in all their needs.

The casualties were :

R.A. Personnel :

1059461 W.O.I. (R.S.M.) Blackett, F. W. J. ...Died of injuries.

1708352 Gnr. Gammon, W. ... ...Seriously injured.

R.E.M.E. Personnel :

7601860 W.O.II (A/Q.M.S.) Cole, G. F. ... Seriously injured.

Home Guard Personnel :

L/Bdr. Wellington, F. G.
L/Bdr. Fishwick, J. H. } All killed.
Gnr. Buckingham, G. J.

Gnr. Kinch, W. S.
Gnr. Houghton, W. G. } Died of injuries.

Lieut. S. C. Gorrell, H. G.
Gnr. Bailey, F. M. } Seriously injured.

Bdr. Grills, H. V.
L/Bdr. Fraser, D. M. } Shock

In recognition of the great sacrifice the dead had made, a full military funeral was ordered and this took place on August 15, 1944, the bodies being interred in the " Heroes' Corner " of the Torquay Cemetery.

The parade assembled at 2-15 p.m. outside the cemetery's main gates and from there, led by a detachment of Royal Artillery, the procession slow marched along the road to the new part of the cemetery. A R.A. band from Southern Command playing the " Dead March " followed the leading detachment.

Then came the gun carriages bearing their coffins draped with Union Jacks. Two lorry loads of wreaths bore silent witness to the tribute being paid.

Following the gun carriages came the cars carrying the relatives and chief mourners, and then came a long khaki procession of military mourners. Among those present were the Sector Commander, Col. H. G. Hay, C.B.E., D.L., representing the Lord Lieutenant of Devon ; the Mayor of Torquay, Mr. E. H. Sermon ; Brigadier J. Wedderburn-Maxwell, D.S.O., M.C., representing Lt.-General W. D. Morgan, C.B., D.S.O., M.C., G.O.C.-in-C. Southern Command ; Brigadier E. T. Weigall, C.C.A., South Western District ; Capt. R. H. Wilson, R.A., representing Brigadier R. J. Wyatt, M.C., T.D., Commander, Devon Sub District ; Major Sir Francis Layland-Barratt, representing South Devon Sector Home Guard ; Lt.-Col. A. J. H. Sloggett, D.S.O., Commanding 10th (Torbay) Bn. Devon Home Guard ; and officers representing the 9th (Newton Abbot), 11th (South Hams) and 13th (Totnes) Bns. Devon Home Guard and many others ; a special detachment of Home Guard gunners and a unit of nearly two hundred Home Guard officers and other ranks.

We buried our dead and saluted them to the sound of the " Last Post," and moved off to fall in once again on the road and march away, past the BRA., to dismiss.

We lived the next four days with the hope in our hearts that others seriously injured would survive, but this was not to be. On August 19 Gnr. Houghton also succumbed to his injuries in the Gloucester City Hospital. We laid him to rest with similar full military honours beside his comrades whom we had buried only nine days before.

A Court of Inquiry sat at once and investigated the whole sad affair, but the exact cause will never be determined. No blame however, attaches to anyone.

To the relatives of those who gave their lives our deepest sympathy ; the dead we will remember with reverence.

" They shall grow not old . . ." We salute the memory of valiant hearts and gallant companions.

The concluding Section of this History is devoted to the names of past and present members of the 10th Battalion

PAST MEMBERS

Compiled from Lists
supplied by Companies

"A" COMPANY

Major
LANDER, F. J.

Captains
CODNER, T. A.
HART, M. G.

Lieutenants
BARTLETT, F. E.
COLLINGS, J., M.M.
POWELL, J. A.

2nd Lieutenants
STAMP, R. G.
SWEETLOVE, A. H.
THOMPSON, W. A.

Sergeants
ARMSTRONG, W. R.
BAKER, A. J.
BOWE, C. T.
COLLINS, H. S.
DUNSFORD, A. G. B.
HEAFEY, E. P.
HILL, R. G.
HILL, J.
HILL, R. W.
HITCHEN, A. L.
HUNTER, N.
KING, F. H.
SHEPHERD, F. R. G.
WIDLAKE, F. E.
WILLS, C. L.
WOOD, E. G.
WORRALL, J.
HAWKINS, N. S.

Corporals
AUSTIN, E. C.
BROOKS, H. H.
CANNING, L. A.
COLLINGS, A. R.
COUZENS, E.
GILL, E.
HANNAFORD, A. B.
HANNAFORD, N. W.
HAWKEN, G. R.
JOHNS, F.
LEWARNE, J. G. W.
LEWIS, F. A.
MATTHEWS, F. R.
NELSON, A. L.
PULLMAN, M. R.
RUSSELL, N. P.
STREETON, H. A.
TOZER, T. P.
VESEY, J. M.
WINDSOR, A. E.

Lance Corporals
BAKER, W. J.
BARTLETT, C. E.
BEVAN, G. E.
BROOME, J. H.
CHALK, G. W.
DEWING, C.C.
DINHAM, J. S.
FIELD, A. A.
GERARD, K.
GILL, A. G.
HALLETT, T. L.
HORTON, R.
HOLLOWAY, A. E.
HYNE, H.

LODGE, T. S.
MATTHEWS, T.
OWEN, W.
OWERS, L. F.
SNOW, F. H.
STEPHENS, A. F.
TAYLOR, L. R.
WATSON, C. T.

Privates
ABBOTT, H. D. S.
AGNEW, T. S.
ALFORD, J. C.
ANDREWS, F. A.
ANDREWS, C.
ANGWIN, J. L.
ATKINS, R. G.
ACTON, A. A.
AGGETT, W. J.
ALLEN, P. L.
ANDREWS, S. R.
ANNEAR, T.
APLIN, E. A.
AVERY, N. C. J.
ADAMS, N. G.
AEDY, K. J.
ALMY, J. P.
ANDREWS, B.
ANNING, A.
ASH, R.

BAILEY, J.
BAILEY, W. G.
BAKER, A. E.
BAKER, A. L.
BAKER, J. W.
BAKER, W. J.
BALL, F. R.
BALL, H. J.
BALSDON, R.
BANDEY, F.
BARTLETT, E.
BARTLETT, C. E.
BATHO, A. E.
BATTEN, R.
BAYLEY, K.
BEARNE, W. A.
BECK, W. T.
BEER, A. T.
BEER, J. W.
BEER, N. H.
BENSON, R. F.
BELL, J.
BENNETT, E.
BENNETT, F. M.
BENNING, P. J.
BENTLEY, C. C.
BERKETT, F. S.
BEST, D. E.
BEVAN, G. E.
BICKLEY, W. S.
BIGNELL, A. E.
BINDON, P. C.
BIRBECK, H.
BLOCKMORE, W. H.
BOCHWIC, M. L.
BOON, E. G.
BOON, T. W.
BODLEY, F. J.
BOND, E. A.
BOND, F. E.
BOND, G. R.
BONING, J. P.
BOVEY, F.
BOWDEN, J. A.

BOWDEN, N. S.
BOYCE, W. J.
BRATCHER, L. J.
BRAY, W. G.
BRETT, N.
BREWER, V.
BRITT, G.
BRITT, R.
BROOKS, H. H.
BROWN, D. E.
BROWN, A.
BROWN, R. E.
BROWN, W. J. S.
BROWN, D. W.
BROWN, E. E. W.
BROWN, J. W.
BROWN, T.
BROWN, W. J.
BROWNE, H. V.
BROWNING, L. V.
BRUCE, I. C. J.
BUDGELL, M. P.
BULLEN, A. E.
BURLEY, E. G.
BURTON, D. E.

CAFFRY, A.
CALVERT, H. G.
CARR-ARCHER, J.
CAMERON, D.
CANN, K.
CAPRON, A. J.
CAPRON, R. M.
CAVANNA, P. M.
CARLTON-STIFF, G. N.
CHADWICK, V. C.
CHALK, R.
CHAPMAN, F. D.
CHAPPLE, W. J.
CHILVERS, .D A.
CHRISTOPHERS, H.
CHRISTIE, R. O.
CLARK, R. T. R.
CLARK, W. T.
CLARKE, A.
CLEMENTS, A. J.
CLOKE, E.
CLOKE, W. G.
CLODE, H. M.
CLOUGH, A. F.
CLEAVE, R. W. A.
COCKING, K.
COGAN, H. T.
COFFEY, L. T.
COLE, H.
COLLINGS, W. L.
COLMAN, W. J.
COOK, B. H.
COURTNEY-DUNN, R. A.
COOK, K. R.
COOKE, J. F.
CORAH, L. A.
CORDLEY, L. B.
CORNISH, C.
CORNISH, I. H.
CORNISH, D.
CORLESS, H. T.
COOMBES, R. J.
COUNTER, A. P.
COUNTER, W. J.
COX, F. N.
COX, A. C.
COWLING, C. S. F.
CRIBBETT, E. C.
CROFTS, A. J.

"A" COMPANY—continued

CROOK, W. J.
CROOT, J. F.
CROSBIE, H. B.
CRUSE, H. J. T.
CUMMING, B. G. G.
DALE, B. E.
DAMERELL, R. L.
DANIEL, C. W.
DAVEY, M. E.
DAVIS, E. W.
DAVIS, J.
DAVIES, D. W.
DAVIES, S. R.
DAMENT, R.
DENBOW, J. A.
DENBOW, R. R.
DENHAM, E. G.
DENMARK, G. A.
DUNN, H. E. J.
DUNNING, R. W. E.
DIXON, G. H.
DOMMETT, P. J.
DIBDEN, L. F.
DILLEY, C. N.
DILLEY, G. W.
DUFFUS, H.
DURRANT, D. E.
DUNTHORNE, G. A.
EARL, E. H. C.
EAST, R. R.
EASTERBROOK, J. D.
EDGECOMBE, H. G.
EDEY, J.
ELLIOTT, F.
ELLIS, G. W.
ERRIDGE, S. W.
ETHERIDGE, W. N.
EVANS, H. F.
EVANS, F. E.
EVANS, J.
EVANS, J. H.
EZRA, D.
FAIRCHILD, E.
FELLOWS, A. G.
FLEET, D. C.
FLETCHER, J. H.
FLINT, L.
FLINT, W.
FORD, G. W.
FORWARD, C. W.
FORTUNE, C. E.
FOSTON, P. W.
FORSTER, J. M.
FOSTER, F. J.
FRANCE, W. W.
FRASER, D.
FULLERTON, N. R.
GAGG, W. R. G.
GARD, C. G.
GAEL, S. M.
GAMBRELL, H. J.
GAME, G. O.
GARDINER, A. W.
GARDNER, J.
GEERE, K. W.
GEORGE, R.
GERARD, W. J.
GIBBINGS, T. H.
GILL, A. J. C.
GILL, A. S.
GILL, E.
GOODYEAR, A. G.
GOULD, T.

GOLDBY, A.
GOLDING, F.
GRAHAM-CLARKE, L. W.
GREEN, F. G.
GREEN, L. M.
GREENER, N. B. S.
GRIMWOOD, C. R.
GUEST, A. E.
HADLEY, J. F. T.
HALL, W. H.
HANLON, F.
HARTLEY, K. J.
HARTLEY, R. J. M.
HARDING, S. R.
HARWOOD, R. F.
HANNAFORD, W. R.
HARVEY, L. C.
HATHERLEY, J.
HATHERLEY, S. E.
HASLETT, J.
HAWKEN, R. S.
HAYES, H.
HAYMAN, C. J.
HAYWOOD, A. F. G.
HEAWARD, E. A.
HEATH, L. N.
HEATH, V. F.
HEMMEL, A. E. D.
HEMMEL, C. E. O.
HERRINGTON, C. H.
HERON, R. V.
HERBERT, C. P.
HEPBURN, R.
HEWITT, C. J.
HICKOX, W. E.
HISCOX, F. G.
HILL, F. C.
HILL, R. G.
HOCKIN, G. L.
HOCKADAY, G. T. E., D.C.M.
HOCKING, H. J.
HOCKINGS, L. J.
HOCKINGS, R. H.
HODGE, A. H.
HODGSON, E. C.
HOGARTH, R.
HOLMAN, K. W.
HOLMAN, L.
HORNBY, H. E.
HOWARD, S. C.
HOWARD, W. H.
HUDSON, W.
HUNT, E. W.
HUGGINS, T. W.
HUTCHINGS, A. H.
HUTCHINGS, W. J.
INGHAM, J. P.
INSALL, W. R.
IREDALE, F. H.
ISHAM, K.
IZZARD, E.
JACKSON, B.
JANES, W. C.
JEPSON, H. W.
JEFFERY, A. O.
JOHNSON, H. W.
JONAS, W. E.
JONES, W.
JOWITT, F. R.
JOHNS, H.
JEPSON, H. W.
JONE, J. T.
KELLOW, J. F.

KELLOW, A. J.
KERR, F. W.
KELLY, D.
KEEVIL, S. P.
KENNY, J. E.
KENTISH, G. E. H.
KEOGH, A. G. P.
KISSER, J.
KNAPMAN, E. H.
LAIDLAY, J. M. L.
LAITY, M. C.
LAMBELL, E. L.
LAMBERT, J.
LANDER, T. S. H.
LANG, T.
LAWRENCE, A. S.
LANGLEY-ELLIS, G. A.
LAX, D. G.
LEACH, C. A.
LEACH, G. F.
LEAMAN, J.
LEGON, C.
LEVY, E.
LOCK, H.
LOCK, R.
LOCKYER, E. V.
LONSDALE, F. D.
LOCOCK, G. J.
LONG, W. H.
LOUDON, H. W. G.
LOW, G.
LOWRY, T. E.
LOSSEMORE, G.
LOXTON, C.
LOXTON, J. C.
LUTON, R. M.
LYDDON, S. G.
MACNAUGHT, W. D.
MARCH, F. J.
MAEERS, F. G.
MAGUIRE, T. H.
MALVERN, M. R.
MANNING, W. J. B
MARTIN, S.
MASSIE, G. B.
MATTHEWS, D. T.
MATTHEWS, E. F.
McCALLUM, R. E.
McCANN, A. S. G.
MANN, E. G.
MARCOVITCH, S.
MARSDEN, J. B.
MARTIN, B. W.
MARTIN, C. W.
MARTIN, I. C.
MARTIN, S.
MATHIESON, F. P.
MATTHEWS, K.
MATTHEWS, L.
MEDHURST, L. M.
MEEK, K.
MELHUISH, C. H.
MELHUISH, F. J.
MADGE, H.
MADGE, W. H.
MAN, E. G.
MARMION, W.
MELHUISH, S. T.
MERRIFIELD, R. J.
MERRIFIELD, G.
METHERELL, D. J.
MILLEDGE, J. S.
MILLER, A. C.
MILLS, F. W. J.
MILLS, G. H.

"A" COMPANY—continued

MILLS, W. G. R.
MILTON, C. R.
MILTON, W. T.
MITCHELL, B. C.
MOONEY, J. G.
MOORE, W. J.
MORGAN, G. B.
MOSS, J. H.
MOSS, V. C.
MOYSER, K. N.
MUNRO, D. F. R.

NETHERWAY, R. G.
NETHERWAY, L. F.
NEW, C. W.
NEWMAN, A. G. H.
NEWTON, I.
NICHOLSON, C. H.
NORMAN, A. E.
NORRISH, E. H. B.
NORTHEY, F. R.

ODDIN-TAYLOR, H.
ORAM, J. H.
OLDHAM, F.
OLDING, A.
ORCHARD, A. E.
OZZARD, W. F.

PACK, S. W. A.
PACKER, J. G.
PADDON, G. H.
PALACE, J. E.
PALMER, L. G.
PALMER, V. G.
PALMER, W. H. R
PARKER, N.
PARNELL, P.
PARNELL, L. W.
PARSONS, C. Q.
PARSONS, C.
PARNELL, R. C.
PARKER, K. S. S.
PARNELL, W. G.
PAYNE, E. F.
PAYNE, S.
PEARCE, C. F.
PEARCE, J. S.
PEARCE, W. G.
PEARSE, C. G.
PEATHEYJOHNS, P. C.
PEEK, F. H.
PEIRCE, R. J.
PEAKMAN, G.
PETHICK, A. F.
PETHICK, H. W.
PERRING, W. E.
PERRING, A. A.
PERRY, C. D.
PHILLIPS, A. T.
PHILLIPS, G.
PHILLIPS, W.
PHILLIPS, W. R.
PHARE, C. P.
PIKE, F.
PISENT, H. J.
PITT, G.
POMEROY, W. H.
POLLARD, W. E. R.
POPHAM, C. H. G.
POPE, N. A.
POTTS, F. G.
PORRIT, R. V.
POTTER, G. H.
POWIS, E. C.
PRICE, J. H.
PROUT, H.

PROWT, H.
PUCKRIDGE, G. E.
PULLHAM, R. J.
PURDEY, H. C.
PYLE, M. C.
PYM, W. A.
QUICK, S. J.
QUICK, W. R.

RADMORE, F.
REDDICLIFFE, A.
REDWOOD, G. F.
REES, G.
REED, A. C.
REESE, A. W. H.
RENDLE, J. G.
RIDD, A. N.
RIDGWAY, J. E.
REYNOLDS, W. J.
RIMMER, W.
RICHARDS, E. F.
RICHARDS, F. P.
RICKETTS, A. E.
ROBERTS, R. J.
ROBERTS, W.
ROBERTSON, W. D.
ROCKETT, F. G.
ROACH, F. R.
RODGERS, R. H.
RODERICK, J.
ROLLINS, R. A.
ROOK, G. S.
ROOK, M. J.
ROOKE, J.
ROOKES, F. S.
ROPER, A. F.
RUSSELL, B. J.
ROWE, C. E.
ROWLEY, E. C. J.
RUSSELL, W.
RUSSELL, W. F.
RYAN, J. A. W.

SANDERS, E.
SANDERS, M.
SAUNDERS, W. G.
SAWYER, J. C.
SCANES, D. H.
SCANES, S. G.
SCOLES, H. J.
SAVAGE, W. F.
SCOTT, J. R.
SHAW, A. J.
SHAW, P. J.
SHEPHARD, F. B.
SHEPHERD, F. R. G.
SHAWCROSS, A. J.
SHEARS, W. H.
SHEPARD, F. T.
SHEPHERD, K. G. H.
SHERRIFF, J. E.
SHERRIFF, C. W.
SHORELAND, F. W.
SKINNER, H. P.
SMERDON, L. G.
SMITH, G.
SLADE, W. E.
SLUGGETT, R. J.
SMITH, E. L.
SMITH, S. N.
SMITH, W. A.
SMYTH, H. E.
SNELLING, R. H.
SNOWSILL, S. H.
SOUTHCOTT, S. F.
SOWDEN, K. A.
SPALDING, T.

SPENCER, T. W.
STACE, R.
STADDON, A. E.
STAPLES, C. A.
STATON, L. J. G.
STEVENS, A.
STILL, L. A.
STOCKMAN, J. W.
STONE, D. M.
STONE, W. C.
STONEMAN, T.
STONEMAN, F. H. V.
STUCKEY, R. H.
SYMONS, J. C.

TARR, D. G.
TAYLER, D. I.
TAYLOR, A. E.
TAYLOR, W. R.
TERRY, W. P.
THORNE, F. J.
THORNE, L. S. J.
THORP, J. P.
TINDALL, F.
TOMMEY, F. W.
TOZER, G. E.
TOZER, T. E.
TRAHAR, N. A.
TRAVERS, J. J
TREBY, H. S.
TREMLETT, R. V.
TROWT, H. J.
TURNER, E. R.
TURNER, F.
TURNER, T. W. G.
TYLER, C. A. W.

UREN, A.

VANSTONE, F. C.
VANSITTART, K. B.
VAREY, J. A.
VESEY, N. M.
VICKERY, W. J. H.
VINCENT, A. G.

WAKEFIELD, T.
WALTER, J. E.
WARD, R.
WARNER, N. S.
WARREN, F. C.
WATSON, P. F.
WATSON, D. K.
WATSON, L. C.
WATSON, M. J.
WATSON, E. E.
WATT, G. W. H.
WEEKS, A. E.
WETHAM, R. J.
WELLS, E. J.
WELLS, P.
WESTLAKE, J. A.
WHELAN, E.
WHARRY, N.
WHIDDON, R. N.
WHITE, F. J.
WHITE, P. G. A.
WHITE, D. J.
WHITE, S.
WHITE, W. J.
WHITNEY, K. P.
WHITEMORE, W. R. G.
WHITTINGTON, A. C.
WHITTINGTON, W. G.
WICKS, W. G.
WILLIAMS, K. J.
WILLIAMS, Y.
WILKINSON, W. E.

"A" COMPANY—continued

WILLIS, W. J.
WILKINSON, W. E.
WILLIAMS, Y.
WILSON, B. S.
WILSON, E. A.
WILSON, R. L. A.
WILSON, R. R. O.
WILSON, W. T. S.
WILSON, T.
WILSON, C.

WEEKS, E.
WINDSOR, L. O.
WINDSOR, C. E.
WINTER, A. R.
WOOD, P. H.
WOOD, D. H.
WOOD, H. C.
WOOD, L. D.
WOODS, M. F. J.
WOOLACOTT, A. B.

WOOLWARD, J. H.
WOTTON, V. W.
WRIGHT, J. W.
WYATT, H. J.
WYNDS, W.

YATES, A.
YATES, C.
YARWOOD, F. G.
YOUNG, F. J.

"B" COMPANY

Major
MOORE, H. R. G., C.B.E.

Captain
EARL, E. H. C.

Lieutenant
DAVIS, S. G., M.M.

Platoon Officers
LEWIS, T. H.
WINSHIP, E. R., M.C.

2nd Lieutenants
GRAHAM, W. H.
GREAVES, H. R. W.
LARKE, E. F.
MORSLEY, H. V.

Sergeants
BRACEWELL, J. H.
CHOWN, H. P.
DUNSFORD, E. H.
HARDCASTLE, J.
JONES, W.
NEWTON, W. A. H.
SANDS, G. E.
SHEPHERD, J.
SQUIRES, H.
VAIL, F. J.
WHITE, G. F. H.
WOOLLIAS, W.

Corporals
BROWNE, R. K.
COLE, F.
DUNCAN, H.
FELTON, S. H.
FIELD, D. C.
HILLMAN, A. E.
HORTON, S.
JAGO, A.
JEFFREYS, O. A.
JENKINS, A. W. T.
JOEL, W. W.
JOHNSON, F. W.
JONES, R. A.
JOWETT, E. B.
JOYES, A.
KENDALL, G. H.
LANG, C. H.
LANGDON, B. R.
MILTON, W. L.
MORTIMER, A.
NORRIS, D. G.
PEARCE, C. H.
SIMS, C.
SWAN, D. G.
THOMPSON, A.

Lance Corporals
BROWN, R. J.
COOK, H.
COOKE, G. G.
CORNISH, H. S.
COURTENAY-DUNN, N. E. A.
GROVES, A. V.
FROMOW, I. A.
HEAWARD, H.
HUNT, R. G.
JENNINGS, W.
KENNEDY, R. D.
LAMONT, H. R.
MILLS, K. H. G.
NEWCOMBE, L. E.
NEWMAN, P. P.
NUNN, G. F.
PYMAN, J. W. A.
WILLIAMS, J. S.

Privates
ABBS, P. H.
ABSOLON, N. H.
ADAMS, H. B.
ADAMS, N. G.
ADDISON, F. H.
ADKINSON, R. H.
ALDRED, S.
ALLBUT, J. W.
ALLCORN, R.
ANDREWS, F. C.
ANDREWS, H. E.
ANDREWS, W. F. J.
ANGELOS, T.
ARCHER, W. T.
ASH, J. H.
ASHTON, J. J.
ATKIN, W. H.
AUDREY, R. H.
AUSTIN, A. E.
AVERY, F. L.
AVERY, P.
BABBAGE, G.
BAKER, W. R.
BARBER, G. S.
BARKER, H. V.
BARNARD, P. J.
BARNES, E. A.
BARNEY, H.
BARTLETT, W. J.
BATE, R.
BATHO, A. E.
BATHE, W. H.
BATTERSHILL, T.
BAWDEN, A. R.
BAY, W.
BAYFORD, S. G.
BEARE, G. N.
BEAZLEY, E. E.

BEAZLEY, H. W.
BECKET, D. J.
BEETON, J. H.
BELL, E.
BENNETT, S. A.
BENSON, A. F. M.
BERRY, C. E.
BERRY, G. T.
BEST, G. R.
BEVAN, E. F.
BILLAGE, J. W.
BIRD, T. P.
BISHOP, D.
BISHOP, D. H. J.
BLACKWELL, L. W.
BLUNT, N. J.
BOARD, D. W.
BOLT, A. R.
BOND, A. G.
BOND, H. P.
BOND, K. J.
BOND, S. T.
BOND, W. C.
BOUNDY, W. C. J.
BOUNEVIALLE, J. A.
BOVEY, A. P.
BOVEY, C. R.
BOVEY, W. N.
BOWDEN, S. A.
BOWDEN, W. H.
BRADFORD, A. T. C.
BRADSHAW, G. C.
BRAME, C. T.
BRAWN, D. H.
BRAY, R. A. H.
BREMRIDGE, K. R.
BRIDGMAN, H. L.
BROCK, A. E.
BROCKWELL, C. F.
BRODERICK, T.
BROOKING, R. R.
BROOKS, A.
BROOKS, H. G.
BROOKS, M. C. W.
BROTHERTON, J. T.
BROWN, A. H.
BROWN, E. N.
BROWN, G. A.
BROWN, J. C.
BROWN, J. P.
BROWN, L. V.
BROWNING, C. A.
BUCHAN, J. D. M.
BURGESS, E. H. V.
BURGOYNE, J. W. E.
BURRIDGE, F.
BURROW, S.
BURTON, A. J.
BUTT, H. G.
BYNE, H. W. E.

"B" COMPANY—continued

BYWAY, M. T. H.

CAHILL, D. W.
CALDER, E. G.
CAMP, J. W.
CAMPBELL, H. P.
CARLETON-STIFF, G. N.
CARR-ARCHER, J.
CARRUTHERS, D.
CASLAKE, T. H.
CAUSLEY, J. P.
CHADWICK, A. G.
CHALK, F.
CHAMBERLAIN, F. C.
CHANDLER, L.
CHAPMAN, R. H.
CHAPMAN, J. T.
CHARLES, J. A.
CHARLES, W.
CHASE, J. E.
CHERRY, C. H.
CHERRY, E. R.
CHIDGEY, R. C.
CHIPMAN, A. W.
CLAIRE, S. A.
CLARE, H. J.
CLARK, B. R.
CLARK, F. R. E.
CLEMENTS, P.
CLEMOW, G. H.
CLOUGH, L. G.
COLES, W.
COLLETT, K. M.
COLLIER, D. M.
COLLING, P. R.
COLLINS, C. F.
COMBER, H. E. D.
CONGRAM, R. J. R.
CONSTANT, A. E.
CONSTANT, R. V.
COOMBE, C. H.
COOMBE, F. H.
COOMBE, P. R.
CORDLEY, L. B.
CORNISH, D.
CORNISH, L. G.
COUNTER, W. J.
COURTHOPE, W. H. F.
COURTIER, C. S.
COWELL, S.
COWHIG, T.
COWLING, W. H.
COWLS, W. H.
COX, F. N.
COX, L.
COYLE, P. J.
CRAYTON, R. R.
CREWS, A. K.
CREWS, E. J.
CROCKER, B. P.
CROCKER, J. D.
CROOK, C. H.
CROOK, J.
CROUCH, R. K.

DAGNELL, J. A.
DAILLEY, C. P.
DALMAN, V. G.
DAMERELL, B. S.
DART, E. J.
DAVEY, E. W.
DAVEY, J.
DAVIDGE, R. G.
DAVIES, C.
DAVIS, C. T.
DAVIS, G.
DAY, G. W.

DEAKINS, W. A.
DENMARK, G. A.
DENT, H. A.
DEWDNEY, F. W.
DICKINSON, J. R.
DINHAM, G. A.
DITCHBURN, G. L.
DIXON, J. F.
DIXON, L. F.
DOBBS, S. J. H.
DOESE, D.
DONEY, H. H.
DOUGLAS, C. S. P.
DOUGLAS, F.
DOUGLAS, G. H.
DOWNER, G.
DOWNING, J. E. F.
DOWNING, P. J.
DRAKE, H. F.
DREW, R. F.
DRURY, F. K.
DUNN, W. H.
DUNSEATH, S. S.

EALES, A. E.
EARWOOD, A.
EARWOOD, R. F.
EASTERBROOK, H. N. C.
EASTERBROOK, R. L.
EDMONDS, W. C.
EDWARDS, H. C.
EDWARDS, J. W. J.
EDWARDS, L. R.
EDWICKER, W.
ELLIOTT, F.
ELLIOTT, J. W.
ELLIOTT, R. D. K.
ELLIOTT, W. E.
ELSON, F. H.
EMERY, C. H.
EMMERTON, A. E.
EMPSON, R. H. W.
ENGLAND, E. T. G.
ENGLAND, H. F.
ENGLAND, S. C.
EVANS, D. I.
EVANS, R. F.

FARLEIGH, D. R. P.
FEARN, H. G.
FEDRICK, J. R.
FEDRICK, S. F. H.
FERGIE, J. S.
FINN, D.
FISHER, W. S.
FLETCHER, R. T.
FORD, L.
FORD, M. F.
FORD, P. H. H.
FRAMPTON, H. W. J.
FRANKLIN, T. H.
FRANKS, C. J.
FRAZER, F.
FREATHY, A. E.
FRENCH, J. F.
FRITH, A. A.
FROST, F. J.
FROST, R. J.
FUNNELL, J. A.

GALE, F. C.
GAVED, L.
GAUGHT, A.
GEE, C. E.
GENT, R. J.
GERMAN, E. M.
GIBSON, J. A. V.

GILBERT, F. E.
GILL, H. C.
GOLLOP, V. R. R.
GOLSBY, J. A.
GOODING, D. R.
GOSLING, B. G.
GOTHARD, L. A.
GOULDEN, A. V.
GRAHAM, F. M.
GRAHAM, W.
GRANT, J. E.
GREEK, W. J.
GREEN, A. H.
GREEN, F. E.
GREEN, R. G.
GRIFFIN, F. H.
GROVER, P.
GUY, A. J.
GUY, A. J. O. C.
GWILLIAM, T. C.

HADDRELL, W. L.
HAGGERD, A.
HALBERT, J. B.
HALE, S. W.
HALES, R. B.
HALFORD, P. H.
HALLETT, S. A.
HAMMETT, J. H.
HANCOCK, R. E. V.
HANSFORD, A. G.
HARDING, H. G.
HARDING, P.
HARDWIDGE, B. G.
HARE, A. J.
HARE, A. W. L.
HARRIS, E. G.
HARRIS, R.
HARRIS, T. S.
HARRIS, W. F.
HART, W. J.
HARTY, E. D.
HARVEY, B. H. A.
HARVEY, G. H.
HARVEY, R. L.
HARVEY, T. W.
HASSELL, M. E.
HARSWELL, L.
HAVILL, E. H.
HAWES, F. M.
HAYLES, R.
HAYMAN, E. G.
HAYMAN, H. G.
HAYMAN, H. W.
HAYMAN, R. J.
HAYMAN, R. JOHN
HAYWARD, G. H.
HEAD, H. S.
HEAL, G. R.
HEARN, N. R.
HENDY, E. T.
HERAPATH, A. W.
HEWETT, C. J.
HEYWOOD, H. S.
HIGGINS, C. F.
HIGGINS, S. J.
HILTON, C.
HIND, S.
HINGSTON, N. E.
HINGSTON, W. N.
HOBBS, A. E.
HOBBS, P.
HOCKING, W. L.
HOCKNEY, N.
HODGSON, J. L.
HOLDING, A. J.
HOLDING, T. H.

"B" COMPANY—continued

HOLLAND, M. J.
HOLLEY, F. W. J.
HOLMES, H.
HOLWILL, F. J.
HONEYBALL, T. G.
HOOPER, A. J. L.
HOOPER, W.
HOPCROFT, R. E.
HOPPER, H. W.
HORSWELL-WILLIAMS, A. E.
HORWILL, W. H.
HOUGHTON, W. G.
HOW, A.
HOWARD, C. L. J.
HOWARD, J.
HOWARD, P. E. L.
HOWELL, R. W.
HOWES, A. F.
HUGGINS, R. J.
HUGGINS, T. W.
HULL, H. L.
HUNT, J. H.
HUSKISSON, C. H.
HUSSEY, F. J.
HUTCHINGS, R. J.
HYHAM, R. C.

IRELAND, H. S.
ISAAC, F. G.
ISAAC, J. R.
ISAAC, W. J.

JACKMAN, C. B.
JACKSON, D. A.
JAMES, C. A.
JAMES, L. H.
JAMES, R. H.
JANES, W. C.
JARVIS, E. J.
JEFFERIES, H.
JEFFREYS, C. A.
JENKINS, J.
JENKINS, R. J.
JENNINGS, M. R.
JERWOOD, W. H.
JESSOP, R. H.
JOHNSON, H. W.
JOHNSON, W. A. C.
JOHNSTONE, F. N. H.
JONES, A. D.
JONES, A. H. D.
JONES, F.
JONES, F. L.
JONES, J.
JONES, T.
JOY, S. E.
JOYES, D. V.
JUDD, G. G. L.
JULIAN, R. T.
JUNG-BURTON, A. A. F.

KEELAN, D. H.
KEEN, H. R.
KEEN, P. E.
KEEN, P. G.
KELLOW, J.
KELLAND, F.
KELSON, A. T.
KELLY, D.
KEMP, M. A.
KENT, B. C.
KEOGH, L. H.
KEYS, H.
KINCH, W. S.
KINDER, R. E. H.
KLINKENBURG, P.
KNEIL, H. F.

KNIGHT, E. C.
KNOWLES, J.
KOOT, W.

LAMBERT, O. Y.
LANE, D. E.
LANE, E.
LANE, S. G.
LANG, R. J. E.
LANGDON, J. C.
LANCASHIRE, H. W.
LASKEY, G. W. D.
LAWRENCE, F. C. P.
LEACH, W. J.
LEAMAN, J.
LEAR, I.
LEE, T.
LEE, W.
LEE, W.
LETTEN, E.
LEWIS, J.
LITTLE, H.
LOOSEMORE, G.
LORRIMAN, A.
LOVE, A. W.
LOVELL, A. S. J.
LOVELL, R.
LOW, S.
LOWE, H.
LUSCOMBE, H.

MACDONALD A
MACLEAN, I. H.
MACPHERSON, D. A.
MALONE, A. J.
MANN, J. W.
MANNING, E. J.
MANTELLO, D. P.
MAPLE, G. G.
MARGETTS, D. W.
MARSHALL, G.
MARTIN, B. W.
MARTIN, G. H.
MARTIN, J. T. H.
MARTIN, R. E.
MARTIN, R. E.
MARTIN, S. H.
MARTIN, W. A
MASON, E. J.
MATHER, H.
MATHEWS, A. T.
MATTHEWS, M.
MATTHEWS, W. J.
MAYDWELL, W. D.
McAULIFFE, D.
McKENNA, R.
McMORRAN, D. R.
MEDHURST, L. M.
MELHUISH, A. F.
MELTON, R.
MERRIFIELD, R. J.
MIDGELEY, J. E.
MILDEN, L. J. S.
MILLER, P.
MILLS, S. J.
MILNE, G. J.
MITCHELL, E. V.
MITCHELL, L.
MOON, R. G.
MOON, R. H.
MOORE, P. G.
MORRIS, R.
MORRIS, R. C.
MORRIS, W. A. T.
MOULSTONE, H. A.
MUDGE, D.
MUDGE, R. E.

MULES, G.
MURDOCH, J. D.

NANKIVELL, F.
NANKIVELL, J.
NARRACOTT, A. G.
NASH-PEAKE, T. H.
NATHAN, R. W.
NATHAN, W. E W.
NEAL, A. E.
NEAVE, B.
NEELS, F. W.
NEVILLE, I. J. B.
NEWBERRY, C. P.
NEWBERRY, J.
NEWBOULD, W. D.
NEWELL, J. D.
NEWTON, W. J.
NEWTON, W. T.
NICHOLS, W.
NICHOLSON, T. W.
NICKELS, G. A. J.
NIGHTINGALE, H. G.
NORCOMBE, F. C. J.
NORTHCOTT, F. J.
NORTHCOTT, F.
NORTON, A.
NORTON, A. R.
NOTLEY, A.

OFFORD, G. E.
O'KEEFE, T.
OLDBURY, A. E.
OLLIVER, H. J.
ORCHARD, F. J. H.

PACK, L. E.
PALK, L. S.
PALLIN, F. J. L.
PALMER, W.
PARKER, T.
PARRY, J. H. J.
PARSONS, J. F.
PASSMORE, P. P.
PAYNE, G. L.
PEARCE, A. G.
PEARCE, W.
PEARCE, W. B.
PEARSON, H. R.
PEEK, F. H.
PENNEY, M. H.
PETERS, H. W.
PHILLIPS, L. J. S.
PHILLIPS, W.
PICKFORD, J. J.
PIKE, G. C.
PIKE, J. R.
PINK, H. A.
PINNEY, A. J.
POAT, A. E.
POLLEY, G. A.
POOLE, G. E. H.
POPE, C.
POPE, D. A.
POPE, K. J.
POPE, R. C.
PORT, A. B.
PORTER, F. W.
PORTER, M. D. J.
POTE, W. G.
POTTER, S. G.
POULTON, J. A.
POUND, J. H.
POWELL, H. C.
PRATT, S.
PRESCOTT, K.
PRETORIUS, P. G,

"B" COMPANY—continued

PRICE, J. H.
PRIESTLEY, J. D.
PROCTOR, R. A.
PROUSE, J.
PROUT, D. F.
PROUT, E. J.
PROWSE, G. H.
PROWSE, A. J.
PUGH, J. C.
PYM, N. E.
PYMAN, W. A. E.
PYNE, J.

RADFORD, C. A.
RADFORD, H. M.
RAISTRICK, V. A.
RATTENBURY, E. W.
RATTENBURY, J. A.
RATTENBURY, W. J.
RAWLE, H.
RAYNER, R. N.
REA, J.
REECE-HILL, B. P.
RENDLE, G. L.
REES, T.
RENNELL, P. G.
RESTORICK, W. C. H.
REEVES, G.
RHOADES, D. E. A.
RICE, G. A.
RICHARDS, W.
RICHARDSON, E. J.
RICHARDSON, P.
RIDER, A. C.
RIDER, A. C. B.
RIDGWAY, J. H.
RIMMER, T.
ROACH, C. F.
ROBBINS, V. E.
ROBERTS, F. J.
ROBERTS, L. F.
ROBERTS, N. J.
ROBERTS, S. F.
ROBERTS, T. A.
ROBINS, H. W.
ROCKETT, A. E. V.
ROCKEY, W. F. J.
RODGERS, W. R.
ROE, A.
ROOKE, G. R.
ROWE, F. J.
ROYCE, L. P.
RUSSELL, S.

SALLIS, H.
SANGSTER, K. A.
SATTERLEY, F. R.
SATTERLEY, W. A.
SATTERTHWAITE, C. W.
SCOTT, F. B.
SCOTT, G.
SCOTT, H. R.
SCOTT, S. H. T.
SCOTT, W. G.
SCOTT, W. J.
SCRAGG, W. H.
SCULLY, E. L.
SEENEY, R. E.
SELLEY, K. J.
SHACKLEFORD, D.
SHANNON, N. L.
SHAPLEY, G. T.
SHAPTER, S.
SHAW, F.
SHAW, R. W.
SHEARS, W. E.
SHEPHERD, A. M.

SHERRELL, L. J.
SHERWOOD, L.
SHINE, D. A.
SIMMONDS, G.
SIMMONDS, G. E.
SIMMONDS, R. C.
SIMS, K. E.
SKINNER, C. C.
SKINNER, J. A. D.
SLEEMAN, P. R.
SLUGGETT, H.
SMALDON, A. E.
SMALE, H. R.
SMITH, D. J.
SMITH, M. C.
SMITH, S. J.
SMITH, W. D.
SMITH, W. H.
SMURTHWAITE, D. I.
SNELL, R. L.
SOMERVILLE, H. H.
SOMERVILLE, W. G.
SOUTHCOTT, A. H. L.
SPARKS, T. W. P.
SPENCER, J.
SPLATT, L. W. K.
SPONG, W. J.
SQUIRE-PERRY, W. H.
STAFFORD, L. S.
STAPLETON, W. G.
STEAD, T. J.
STEELE, A. J. R.
STENTIFORD, L. T. H.
STEPHENSON, A. J.
STERRY, R.
STEVENS, F. G.
STEVENS, R.
STEVENS, R. P.
STEWART, D. B.
STIDWORTHY, C.
STOCKWELL, H. C. R.
STONE, W.
STONEHAM, K. M.
STUCKEY, G.
SWAYNE, M. H.
SWEENEY, B.
SWIFT, P. R.

TANNER, E.
TAYLOR, D. M.
TAYLOR, E. W. G.
TAYLOR, F.
TAYLOR, W. H.
THOMAS, A. R.
THOMAS, J. R.
THOMAS, W. J.
THORNTON, W. J.
THUMPSON, N. S.
TIDRIDGE, P. R.
TILLBROOK, P. H.
TIPPETT, W. G.
TITLEY, A.
TOLLEY, W. T.
TOLLIDAY, F. H.
TOUT, F. R.
TOUT, K. O.
TOUT, M.
TOWELL, G. W.
TOWELL, H.
TOZER, C.
TOZER, C. E.
TOZER, N. R.
TRAND, R.
TREBY, W. F.
TRIANCE, L. M.
TRUMAN, G.
TUCKER, H. E.

TUCKER, L.
TUCKER, V. G. H.
TURK, J. A.
TURNER, M. E. W.
TURNER, T. W.
TWINE, C. E.
TWINING, W. T.
TYRELL, H.

UNDERHILL, P. L.
UZIEL, M. R.

VAKIL, N. P.
VAKIL, S.
VEITCH, E. E. A.
VINCENT, D. A.
VINCENT, H. S.

WADSWORTH, W.
WAKEHAM, F. C.
WALKER, A. J. P.
WALLACE, D. S.
WARREN, K. F.
WATKINS, J. G.
WATTS, C.
WATTS, M. L.
WATTS, N. J. T.
WAY, I. J.
WAYMOUTH, C. H.
WEBSTER, H.
WEDDELL, G. F.
WEEKS, M. W.
WEEKS, W. H.
WEEKS, W. J.
WEEKS, A. E. J.
WEISS, C.
WELLINGTON, L. H.
WELLS, E. S. J.
WELSH, T. E.
WHEATON, N. H.
WHITE, D. H.
WHITE, H. O.
WHITE, P. G. A.
WHITE, S. J.
WHITE, W. G.
WHITLEY, E.
WHITEMORE, G.
WHITNEY, K. P.
WIDDICOMBE, T. A.
WIGGINS, P. J.
WILKINSON, A. F.
WILKINSON, W. F.
WILLIAMS, E. S.
WILLIAMS, F.
WILLIAMS, G. F.
WILLIAMS, H. J.
WILLIAMS, H. T. I.
WILLIAMS, L. O.
WILLIAMS, W. O.
WILLS, L. G.
WILSON, D. H.
WILSON, E. A.
WILSON, J. A.
WINSER, B.
WINSLADE, E. T.
WINSTONE, W. J.
WINTER, A. R.
WOOD, A. C.
WOOD, B. F.
WOOD, H. A.
WOODWARD, J.
WOOLLAND, W.
WORMERSLEY, C. H.
WORTH, F.
WRAYFORD, R. G.
WYNNE, W. F.

YELLAND, W. L.
YOUNG, C. H.

"C" COMPANY

Lieutenant
KING, T. W.

2nd Lieutenant
DENNING, D. E.

Sergeants
FINCH, R. P.
JONES, F. L.
PAPWORTH, S. W.

Corporals
BRUNNING, H. W.
BRIDGES, D. H.
SHEPPARD, H.
WARD, W. C.

Lance Corporals
COLE, J. J.
FROST, W. J.
FARRELL, J. R.
HENSON, R. R.
HARRIS, G. I. J.
HEXTER, W. T.
LORRIMAN, A.
LANGLEY, W. E.
WALKER, F. C.

Privates
AUSTIN, F.
AGGETT, G.
AVERY, O. C.
ABLE, B. J. F.
ALMOND, W. J.

BROOKING, P. J.
BUSE, L. D.
BUCKLAND, N.
BOWYER, C. J.
BROOKING, P.
BIGNALL, J. R.
BOYNE, J. P.
BLIGHT, G. E.
BERTRAM, E. G.
BURROWS, R.

COCKER, K. J.
CARTER, F.
COLLINGS, W. F.

CORNELIUS, G. W.
COLES, J.
CROOK, L. W.
CHEVES, P. B.
CLARK, F. J.
COOPER, S. A.
CANNELL, F.

DENYER, C. F. J.
DENYER, W.
DEARLOVE, W. E.

ELLIS, J. H.
ELLIOTT, S. J. V.
EASTMENT, A. G.
ELLIS, A.
EDWORTHY, C. H.

FURZEMAN, C. W.

GORE, T.
GURNEY, J. G.
GREGORY, T. S.
GULLY, J.
GREEN, R. G.
GERMAN, P.

HOPKINS, A. E.
HANCOCK, W.
HOLGATE, T. R.
HOLMES, L. H. R.
HUMPHREYS, E. G.
HAYNES, E. J.
HARRIS, T. L.
HADDY, J. F.
HILL, J. T.

JORDAIN, E.

KINGSLAND, J. C. P.

LUGG, M. T.
LUCKHAM, D. A.
LAMBLE, G.
LANDESBURG, R. J.
LANGDON, C. D.
LOVATT, G. E.
LEGG, J. T. H.
LEACH, C. D.

MAUNDER, J. H.
MATTHEWS, H. J.
MAY, W. J.
MATTHEWS, W. M.
MITCHELL, D. C.
MACGREGOR, J.
MEAD, W. C.
MARSHALL, W.
MIDDLETON, F. J.
MEDLAND, H. D.

POTTINGER, L.
PAYNE, A.
PERRY, W. G.
POWELL, H.
PENWARDEN, G. W.

QUICK, P. R.
QUILLEY, D. F.

REED, L. O.
REVELL, P. J. H.
RALPHSON, H.

SEXTON, J.
SETCHFIELD, H. P.
SEAWARD, W. H.
STEPHENS, Z. C.
SOLOWEICZYK, L. M.
SEYMOUR, V.
STONE, C. S.
STROUD, P. N.

TUCKER, W. E.
THOMAS, R.
TUCKER, T. J.
TOZER, B.
THURSTAN, N. M. C.
THORNE, M.

WILLIAMS, W. H.
WIDDICOMBE, S. A.
WILLS, P. W. F.
WEBBER, S. G.
WILLICOTT, W. T.
WILLIAMS, N. H.
WOTTON, W. C. M. S.
WINSOR, A. W.

"D" COMPANY

Major
PARSONS, W. L.

Captains
CUNNINGHAM-SMITH, M. O.
FIELD-FISHER, C. H.
HAY MATTHEW, B
SNELSON, J. T.

Lieutenants
McALLISTER, S. C.
MONTGOMERY, R. B.
NORTHEY, G. B. O.
PAUL, H.
SYMONS, H. H.

Platoon Leaders
EVANS, H.

GLENN, H. W.

A/Sergeant Major
VIRGO, H. W.

A/Q.M.S.
CLAYTON, L. K.

C.Q.M.S.
CONNOR, W. G.

Sergeants
DENNY, P. R. A.
HERBERT, F. H.
JAMES, P. S.
MOGRIDGE, J. D.
PRATLEY, G. W.
SHEPARD, E. R.

TRACEY, I. L.
WILLIAMS, F. H.
WINSOR, E. A.

Corporals & Bombardiers
BATT, C. K.
BECKENHAM, R. F.
DART, E. G.
HANNAFORD, F. E.
HAZLEWOOD, S. J.
HOPKINS, G.
TUCKERMAN, W.
TUDEMAN, C. A.
WAKEHAM, R. E.

L/Corporals & L/Bombardiers
DAVEY, D. C. E.
DOIDGE, F. W.
GILES, R. F. A,

"D" COMPANY—continued

HOLLOWS, W. E.
JACKMAN, W. H.
KNIGHT, E. G.
NEAL, R. S.

Privates & Gunners
ALLERY, E. G.
ANDREWS, E. G.
ANSELL, A.
ASH, C. F.
ASH, J. R.
ASH, E. G.
ASH, A. G.
ASH, E. S.
ASHFORD, E.

BAKER, J.
BALSDON, C. J.
BAMBERRY, W. H.
BANDY, C. J.
BARTLETT, J. C.
BARTLETT, E. J.
BASTIN, V.
BATTERSHALL, A.
BAWDEN, W. W.
BEAUMONT, W. D.
BEAUMONT, A. G.
BEER, A. G.
BEER, L. J.
BERRY, H. H.
BINHAM, S. G.
BIRD, G.
BLACKMORE, F. W.
BLAGDON, F. W. G.
BLAGDON, F. C.
BLAGDON, D. R.
BLAKE, T. H.
BLENKIN, T. S.
BLAGDON, R.
BLOWERS, J. G.
BOOLS, H. A.
BOON, W. L.
BOVEY, A. C.
BOWLES, T.
BRADDEN, E.
BRADFORD, L. T.
BRANDON, C. V.
BRAZIER, A. H.
BREMBRIDGE, K.
BRIDGE, W. A. S.
BROKENSHIRE, T. C.
BUBEER, B.
BELL, G.
BULLEN, W. J. L.
BULLEY, P.
BURRIDGE, E. J.
BURRIDGE, R. F.
BURNARD, K. E.
BYRNE, R. G.
CHARLES, F. N.
CHILD, F. H.
CHIVERS, H. A.
CHURCHILL, J. E.
CHURCHILL, J. S.
CHAMBERLAIN, T.
CLAXTON, A. H.
CLAY, E.
CLAYTON, H. D.
CLIFT, C. H.
CLIFT, G.
COATES, T. H.
COLE, G. H.
COLLIER, L. W.
COLEMAN, P. D. S.
CONNELL, F. G.
CONNELL, I. H.
COOMBE, R. F.

COOMBES, J. H.
COOPER, G. E.
COOPER, S. H.
CORBAULD, P. S.
CORDER, A. H.
CORNHILL, A. E. B.
CORNISH, F.
COTSELL, E. P.
COYSH, W. S.
CRANG, H.
CROCKER, B. C.
CUDD, N.
CUMMING, C. H. R.
DALTON, J. A.
DAVEY, A. H.
DAVEY, A. F.
DAVIE, W. J.
DAVIES, J. R. M.
DAVIES, D. L.
DAVIES, R. D.
DAVIES, A.
DAVIS, H.
DEARSON, H. P.
DEARSON, E. A.
DERGES, J. A.
DESMOND, J. T.
DEXTER, A.
DIX, F. W.
DODD, C. D.
DODD, C. B.
DOUGLAS, P. T.
DOWELL, V.
DOWN, J.
DREW, F. A.
DYER, W. H.
DYER, G. H.

EARNSBY, A. E.
EASTON, P. V.
EDMONDSON, R. E.
EELS, W.
EVANS, E.
EVANS, J.
EVELEIGH, W. J.
FEATHERSTONE, K. A.
FEATHERSTONE, W. B.
FOULGER, C. A.
FOWLER, R. G.
FRADD, E. T.
FREER, H. A.
FIELDS, S.

GAY, L. F.
GALLOWAY, W. C.
GARDNER, F. C.
GEDDES, J.
GEORGE, E. G.
GIFFARD, E.
GLANVILLE, F. B.
GOSS, R. J.
GOULDSMITH, A.
GREEN, A. J.
GREEN, H.
GREENLAND, C. A.
GREGORY, C. H.

HALL, S. B.
HALL, H. G.
HAMLING, R. R. L.
HANNAFORD, E. J.
HANNAFORD, H. E.
HARRINGTON, W. J.
HARRIS, E.
HARRIS, S.
HARRIS, S. J.
HART, A.
HART, G.

HARVEY, G. H.
HARVEY, W. J.
HARWOOD, A. W.
HAY, G. B.
HAYES, B.
HAYMAN, J.
HAYMAN, F. E.
HAYWOOD, G. B.
HEAD, S.
HELLEY, D. A.
HELLEY, R. J.
HELLEY, R. S.
HELLEY, V. G.
HELLYER, C. M.
HEATHERINGTON, F. H.
HEWSON, L. S.
HICKS, F. C.
HILL, A. H.
HICKS, D.
HICKS, C.
HILL, W. E.
HINGSTON, F. C.
HOCKEY, J. J.
HOCKINGS, W. D.
HOCKINGS, W. H.
HOLLAND, N. H.
HOLM, M. D.
HOWE, H. J.
HORSLEY, E. B.
HOSKINS, J. C.
HUNT, W. L.
HUSSON, J. R.
HUTCHISON, G. D.

ISAAC, H. E.
IVEY, W.

JACKMAN, E. A.
JAMES, R. J. T.
JARVIS, G. I.
JARVIS, V. P.
JOHNS, W. H.
JONES, F. W. D.
JORDEN, T. H.

KELWAY-BAMBER, H.
KENNAR, S. G.
KIMBLE, R. J.
KIMBLE, S. D.
KING, C. M.
KINGHAM, F. J.
KINGSBY-HUNTLEY, D.
KINGSCOTE, E. T.
KNOTT, W. C.
KNOWLES, G. W.
KNOWLES, J. A.
KYFFIN, J. T.
KEEFFE, F.

LAMSWOOD, F.
LAWLEY, G. H.
LEE, M.
LEE, S. W.
LEVETT, F. S.
LEY, G. J.
LIDSTONE, W.
LIGHT, S.
LIGHT, A. G.
LISSAHER, R. B.
LLEWELLYN, A. D. G.
LLEWELLYN, E. H.
LONGTHORPE, B. H.
LORAM, S. C.
LORAM, R.
LORAM, W. J.
LOVETT-CAMERON, H. F.
LOWE, W.

"D" COMPANY—continued

LUPTON, D.
LUXTON, W. J.
McCORMACK, W. O. X.
MAJOR, A. J.
MALLOWAN, M. E. L.
MARCH, H. N.
MARDON, E. J.
MARSHALL, K.
MARTIN, A. H.
MARTIN, L. E.
MARTIN, J.
MARTIN, S. H.
MATTHEWS, S. F. W.
MAY, T. G.
McDONALD, J. G.
MEDWAY, P. V. V.
MEYER, E. V.
MILLARD, G. T. E.
MILLS, S. S.
MILLS, F.
MINNS, W. W. C.
MOGRIDGE, H.
MOORE, F. C.
MOXEY, F.
MURRAY, A. M.

NEWTON, R.
NICHOLL, C. E.
NICHOLLS, A. W.
NOCK, G. A.
NOLAN, J. T. H.
NORTH, H. W.

OLIVER, F. E.
OSBORNE, F.
OAKLEY, E. T.

PACK, K. C.
PACK, L. E.
PACK, C. W. E.
PALMER, F.
PALMER, E. C.
PARKER, J. T.
PARKER, R. A.
PARNELL, H. H.
PARNELL, S. H.
PARTRIDGE, E. L.
PARTRIDGE, P. G.
PARTRIDGE, W. H.
PATEMAN, A. F.
PERCY, F. E.
PERY-KNOX-GORE, E. A.
PHILIPS, W.
PIPER, R. J.
PITMAN, L. S.
POCOCK, R. G.
POLSON, W. H.
POMEROY, C. H.

POOK, N. J.
POTTER, H.
POYNTER, W. G.
PRESTON, W. J.
PRICE, J. P.
PRINCE, H. A.
PUTT, E. J.
PUTT, W. S.
PUDDICOMBE, F. J.

RACKLEY, W. J.
RADMORE, H. J.
REYNOLDS, C. H.
RICE, S. J.
RICKARD, A.
RICKARDS, C. A.
ROBERTSON, G.
ROCKEY, F. T.
ROCKEY, W. W.
RODBOURNE, F.
ROFFEY, J. C.
ROGERS, H. C.
ROWLAND, R.
RUMP, L. A.
RUSSELL, H. A.
RUSSELL, H. A.
RUSSELL, G. A.
RUTTLEDGE, H.

SALISBURY, K.
SALISBURY, F. A.
SALISBURY, R.
SALISBURY, H. C.
SALISBURY, R. H. B.
SALISBURY, H.
SALMON, E. C.
SANDERS, J. H. K.
SARAH, A. J. K.
SCOBLE, W. G.
SCOTT, R. J.
SCOTT, P. P.
SHARP, C. J.
SHAW, C. A.
SHEPARD, R. G.
SHERRIFF, H.
SHIPLEY, F.
SHRIVES, W. E.
SHRIVES, W. H.
SIMMONS, J.
SLOMAN, T. G.
SMITH, J. B.
SPURWAY, W. S.
SQUIRES, A. J.
SQUIRES, H. A.
STAMP, F. J.
STANBRIDGE, G. E.
STAPLETON, B.
STAPLETON, R. R.

STAPLETON, H. W.
STEVENS, J.
STOCKMAN, S. H.
STOKES, W. C. W.
STRINGER, J. A.

TABB, J.
TABB, S. W.
TAIT, W. S.
TALBOT, E.
TAMLIN, F. A.
TASKER, R. V.
TAYLOR, E.
TAYLOR, S. G.
TERRY, W.
THOMAS, C. R.
THOMAS, F. D.
THOMPSON, W. J.
THOMPSON, J. O.
THOMPSON, A. L.
TOOLEY, R. A.
TOZER, R.
TREMLETT, C.
TRUST, H.
TRYDELL, F. R.
TUCKERMAN, C.
TYACK, H. S.
TURNER, J.

UNDERWOOD, W. F.

VINCENT, S. J.

WADE, W.
WALKER, H. A.
WARD, H. H.
WARREN, J.
WATSON, J. H.
WESTCOTT, K. D.
WESTCOTT, C.
WEYMOUTH, F. T. J.
WEYMOUTH, J.
WEYMOUTH, E. J.
WHITE, C. J.
WHITE, E.
WIDDICOMBE, A. N.
WIDDICOMBE, F. R.
WILLCOCKS, D. T.
WILLIAMS, W. C.
WILLIAMS, L. H.
WILLIAMS, S. F.
WILLIAMS, W. J.
WINSOR, S. H.
WOOLSTON, F. S.
WORTH, G.
WOTTON, V. P.
WOTTON, W. C.
WRIGHTON, F.

YOLLAND, J. S.

"F" COMPANY

Majors
GRANSMORE, F. W.
WOOSLEY, E. H., O.B.E.

Lieutenants
ALLDAY, R. C.
BOWEN, A.
CREE, A. McM.
FITZGERALD, M. C.
GREGORY, P. W. J.
HUNTER, T. S.
LUPTON, D.

McCLATCHIE, N. H.
McDONALD, C.
McLELLAN, C. D. J.
McMILLAN, J.

2nd Lieutenants
COULDREY, H. M.
EARL, E. A.
JEWELL, H. W.
MONTGOMERY, T. A.
RENNIE, C. R.
WILKINSON, H. C.

C.S.M.
LEWINS, C. A.

Sergeants
BAKER, A. E.
BUCKLEY, H. G.
DREW, C. W.
ELLIS, G. S.
GEAKE, A. W.
LEVICK, F. C. T.
SCARR, A. H.
YALLAND, L. J.

"F" COMPANY—continued

Corporals
BLACKMORE, W. S.
BRUNNING, H. W.
CROCKER, F.
DAVIES, C. S.
HEAL, A. J.
JORDAN, L. J. J.
MAIN, B. C. H.
NICHOLAS, F. J. C.
POTTINGER, E. B.
RYDER, S. R. S.
SADLER, M. J.
SKINNER, O. O.
STIDWORTHY, G. H.
SWAN, N. A.
WEBBER, W. G.

Lance Corporals
BAKER, C. M.
COLLINGS, C. F.
COOKSLEY, R. G.
FURNEAUX, W. E.
GANE, W. M.
GILLARD, W. A.
HILL, E. O.
HILL, J. A.
HODGE, C.
HORSHAM, P. G. (Jr.)
LUCKHAM, R. C. G.
PASCOE, E.
SOPER, R.
WEBB, R.
WEBB, V. G.
WEBBER, P. J.
WRIGHT, F. J.

Privates
ABBOTT, W. F. B.
ADAMS, D. A.
ADAMS, F. W.
ADAMS, H. F.
ADLEY, J. B.
ALLAN, H. W. S.
ALLWOOD, F. T.
ANDREWS, G. F.
ANDREWS, R. C.
ANTHONY, R. R. L.
ASH, A. E.
AUTHERS, W. S.

BADCOCK, H. G. A.
BAILEY, G. E.
BAKER, A. R.
BAKER, B. J.
BAKER, L.
BAKER, S. S.
BAKER, T. I.
BALLINGER, K. C.
BALSDON, A. J.
BALSDON, J. C.
BAMSEY, R. W.
BARKER, G.
BARNES, R. W.
BARTLETT, F. G.
BARTON, J. F.
BASHFORD, K.
BASTIN, L.
BATCHELOR, E.
BATEMAN, H. J.
BATES, H. J.
BATH, S. P.
BATTERSHELL, W. R.
BAXTER, W. B.
BEER, C. H. J.
BEER, E. A.
BENNETT, A. H.
BENNETT, R. S. N.

BERRY, W. J.
BERRYMAN, F. W. A.
BERRYMAN, W. S. E.
BEST, F. A.
BILBY, W. J.
BILLINGE, W. F. H.
BINMORE, R.
BINMORE, W. A.
BIRD, C.
BISHOP, D.
BLACKMORE, H.
BLACKMORE, L. B.
BLAIR, J.
BLAKE, S. H.
BLANK, D. H.
BLANK, R. H.
BOND, H. J.
BORER, S.
BOWDEN, F. A.
BOWDEN, J.
BOWRON, W. F. H.
BOWYER, C. J.
BOYD, A.
BOYLE, W.
BEADFORD, G. R.
BRAGG, D. G.
BRAILEY, C.
BRAILSFORD, F. W.
BRATCHER, W. H.
BRAUND, J. O.
BRIDLE, G.
BRITTAIN, N.A.
BRITTAN, W.
BROWN, G.
BROWN, J.
BROWN, P. D.
BROWN, R. T.
BROWN, S.
BROWN, W. A.
BULLEY, A. E.
BUNKER, T. H.
BURRIDGE, W. R.
BURTON, C. H.
BUTLAND, J. H.
BUTLER, B. S.
BUTTERWORTH, H.
BUTTERWORTH, R. E.

CALLARD, C.
CALLEN, H. V.
CAMPION, L. W. J.
CAREY, F. A.
CHEETHAM, H.
CHUBB, J. W.
CHURCHWARD, C. G.
CHURCHYARD, J. P.
CLARE, E.
CLARK, A. J.
CLARKE, J.
CLEAR, J. M.
CLINCH, A. E.
COATH, G. H.
COCKER, K. J.
COLE, A. C. I.
COLE, W. A.
COLES, C.
COLLACOTT, R. T.
COLLINGS, A. W.
COLLINGS, G. J.
COLLINGS, H.
COLLINGS, T. R.
COOK, D. C.
COOK, H. H.
COOPER, A. J.
COOPER, S. C.
CORBETT, H.
CORNISH, W.

CORRICK, P.
CORY, J.
COTTER, J.
COULSON, A. G.
COWLING, G. H.
COX, L. E.
CRABB, K. A.
CRATHORN, J. J.
CRIMP, F.
CRISPIN, J. L.
CROCKER, C. F.
CROOK, C. H.
CROOK, G. P.
CROSS, H. J.
CROSS, W. J.
CROUCH, W. A.
CRUDGE, W. J.
CURTIS, W. J.

DALE, W. C.
DAMARELL, S. E.
DAMMARELL, J. W.
DAVEY, J. A.
DAVIES, C.
DAVIES, T. P.
DAVIS, C. H.
DELVOE, F. P.
DENNIS, J. F. C.
DENNIS, R.
DERGES, R.
DICK, A.
DOBLE, J.
DODD, G. J. J.
DOMINEY, L. G.
DOWELL, M. J.
DOWN, B. E.
DUCIE, H. W.
DUFFUS, G. S.
DUNSTON, G. E.

EAST, R. G.
EDWARDS, S.
EDWORTHY, D. J.
EKERS, H. F.
ELEY, G. W.
ELLIOTT, F. L.
ELLIOTT, J. W. G.
ELY, S. L.
EMERSON, R. J.
EMMERSON, G. W.
EMMERSON, W. A.
ENGLAND, R. H. S.
EWAN, H.

FELLOWES, T. R.
FIELDING, H. H.
FINCH, L.
FINNING, R. G.
FLEMING, W. H.
FLETCHER, F. R.
FLETCHER, S. W.
FORD, K.
FOREMAN, L. B.
FOSTER, D. S.
FOSTER, H. H.
FOSTER, W. H. H.
FOOT, W. L.
FOOTNER, H. F.
FRANCIS, G. W.
FRANKLIN, R. A. E.
FRENCH, L. J.
FRIEND, L.
FRY, E. H.

GABB, C.
GALE, M. L.
GANT, W.

"F" COMPANY—continued

GAYTON, L. F.
GEENS, L. I.
GEORGE, A. P.
GERRARD, W. L.
GIBBS, J. R.
GILBERT, C. H.
GILES, H. A. T.
GILLE, R.
GODDARD, A. E.
GOODWIN, D. C.
GORE, K. C.
GOULD, E.
GOULD, G. J.
GOWMAN, R. H.
GRANT, D. S.
GRANT, F. J. L.
GRANT, S.
GREEN, H. D. E.
GREENHOUGH, V. J.
GREGORY, W. H.
GRISTWOOD, R. D.
GUISE, J.
GUTTERIDGE, E. N.
GUYMER, R. H.
GYNN, H. J.

HAKES, F.
HAKES, P.
HALL, T.
HANNAFORD-HILL, W.
HARDING, F. J.
HARLEY, W. F.
HARRIS, R. E.
HARRIS, S. G.
HART, H. T.
HARVEY, E. W.
HARVEY, L. J.
HARWOOD, F.
HASELWOOD, G.
HATTERSLEY, A.
HAVILL, H.
HAWKESWORTH, P.
HAWKINS, E. S.
HAWTRY, G. H. C.
HAYCOCKS, D.
HAYES, P. J.
HAYNES, H.
HAYWARD, A.
HAYWARD, C. E.
HEAL, J. W.
HEALING, R. H.
HEATH, A.
HEATH, R.
HEARD, A. J. P.
HEARD, F. W.
HEARD, H.
HEEKS, N.
HELLIER, F. P.
HENNESSY, J. G.
HENNESSY, R.
HENVILL, L. J.
HENVILLE, W. J.
HERSOM, S. E.
HESELTINE, C. D.
HEYWOOD, V. R. I.
HILL, D.
HILL, F. D.
HILL, F. J. H.
HILLIER, H. J.
HINE, F.
HINE, R. E.
HINGSTON, H.
HISCOCK, W.
HODSON, T.
HOLDER, A. L.
HOLMES, T. V.
HOMER, R. E.

HOOPPELL, E. G.
HORRY, C.
HORSWELL, T. S.
HORWOOD, V. W.
HUDSON, P.
HULL, E. R.
HUNTER, S.
HUSSEY, W.
HUTCHINGS, H. S.

JACKSON, L. E.
JACOB, C. W.
JAMES, B. F.
JARVIS, F. J.
JEFFERIES, A. H.
JEFFERIES, E. J.
JENKINS, A. C.
JOBLIN, E.
JOHNS, G. H. C.
JOHNS, W. R.
JOHNSON, F. J.
JOHNSON, H.
JOHNSON, S. B.
JOHNSON, W. E.
JONAS, J. H.
JONAS, P. J.
JONES, B.
JORDAN, L. J. J.
JUDD, A. E.

KEENAN, H. J.
KELLAWAY, F.
KENNEDY, E. G.
KENNEDY, E. H.
KENNY, H. H.
KENYON, S. N.
KERSLAKE, L. G.
KERSWELL, L. H.
KING, E. P.
KITCHEN, W.
KITSON, A.
KNAPMAN, B.
KNAPMAN, G. W.
KNIGHT, N. B.
KNOWLES, S.

LAMB, H. W. K.
LAMBLE, K. A.
LANE, C. A.
LANE, W. T.
LANGDON, G. L.
LEADER, J.
LEAR, R. G.
LEAVER, J.W.
LEESON, J. R.
LEMON, R. C.
LEMON, W. A. T.
LETHBRIDGE, L. T.
LEWIS, C. C.
LEWIS, W. G.
LIDSTONE, J. L. E.
LINSCOLL, E. J. C.
LLOYD, W. E.
LODDIE, W.
LOWE, P. G.
LOWMAN, P. R.

MACE, A. J.
MACHIN, F. P.
MACKAY, W. G.
MAHANY, K. W.
MALCOLMSON, B.
MAPPIN, H.
MARKS, G. H.
MARLES, E.
MARSHALL, W.
MARTIN, P. D.

MASON, D. H.
MASSER, A.
MATTHEWS, L. C.
MAUNDER, H. A.
MAUNDER, J. A.
MAUNSELL, R. B.
MAY, P. N.
MAYERS, E. H.
McCALL, J.
McKENZIE-HALL, J. E.
McNULTY, W.
MEAD, P. W.
MILES, S.
MILFORD, F. J.
MILLAR, J.
MILLIS, J. F.
MILWARD, J. A. F.
MITCHELL, C. J.
MITCHELMORE, C. A.
MITCHELMORE, R. C. J.
MOORE, H. R.
MOREY, R.
MORGAN, A. D. G.
MORTIMORE, C. H.
MORTIMORE, W. L.
MOSLEY, T. W.
MOUNTSTEVENS, H. C. E.
MOYSEY, F. J.
MUGFORD, H. H.
MUGFORD, N. C.
MULLET, E. G.
MURCH, H. R.
MURSON, E.
MUXWORTHY, R. H.

NEIGHBOUR, E. H.
NELDER, D. R.
NELDER, D. R.
NELDER, W. H.
NEWBOULD, J. F.
NICHOLSON, H. G.
NORTHCOTT, F.
NORTHCOTT, W. H.

O'BRIEN, C. P.
OLIVER, H. J.
ORCHARD, H. C.
OSBORNE, F. J.
OSBORNE, J. E.
OWENS, C. W.

PAGE, C. H.
PALMER, A. W.
PANTER, A. J.
PARKER, G. E.
PARKIN, W. R.
PARNELL, K. R. H.
PARTINGTON, J.
PASSELLS, A. G.
PAYNE, S. C.
PAYNE, W. H.
PEARCEY, W.
PEARSE, F. W.
PEARSE, H.
PEARSE, S. T.
PEEL, C. D.
PELOSI, E.
PELOSI, J. B.
PELOSI, P.
PENNELL, F. R. C.
PENWARDEN, G. W.
PERRAM, P.
PHELPS, P. W. C.
PHILLIPS, F.
PHILLIPS, S. J.
PICKARD, H. S.
PICKARD, R.

"F" COMPANY—continued

PICKARD, T.
PIKE, S. A.
PILE, F. C.
PILE, H. A.
PINE, G. E.
PIPER, C.
PIPER, R. G.
PITMAN, S. H.
PITTWOOD, J.
POMEROY, R. F.
POPE, G. R.
POPPLESTONE, P.
PORTER, A. J.
POTT, F. W.
POTTER, P.
POWELL, H.
PRINCE, G. R. I.
PRISK, S.
PROSSER, R. C.
PROSSER, R. T.
PULLIN, J. J. B.

REED, W. T. V.
REYNOLDS, H. J.
REYNOLDS, J. C.
REYNOLDS, W. A.
RICE, A.
RICHARDS, G.
RICHARDS, J. M.
RIPLEY, E. J.
ROACH, F.
ROBBINS, C.
ROBERTS, C.
ROBSON, C.
ROE, H.
ROE, N. S.
ROGERS, C. H.
ROLLINS, G.
ROSE, J. J.
ROWE, G.
ROWE, S. D.
ROWELL, E. G.
ROWELL, E. J.
ROWELL, J.
ROWLAND, C. F. J.
ROWLANDS, E. W.
ROWLEY, P. G.
RUTTER, F. J.
RYDE, J. E.

SALTER, A. T.
SALTER, L.
SALTER, W. M.
SANDERS, D. G.
SANDERS, F. M. W.

SAUNDERS, G. C.
SAWYER, R. M.
SERCOMBE, R. T.
SHEARS, A. J.
SHEARS, K. R.
SHEPPARD, A. C.
SHRUBSOLE, F.
SIBLEY, A.
SIMKINS, F. W.
SIMMONS, E. T. B.
SKINNER, H. J.
SLATER, T. C.
SLOOMAN, C. J.
SMYTH, T. C.
SNELL, F. G.
SOUTHWOOD, R. S.
SPRAGUE, S. M.
STADDON, D. J.
STADDON, J.
START, J.
STEVENS, E. J.
STEVENS, J. B.
STIDWORTHY, W. G.
STOCKMAN, F. G.
STOCKMAN, R. H.
STONE, J.
STONELAKE, C. G.
STOYLE, W. D.
STRANGER, F.
STUART, J.
STURROCK, A. R.
SYMS, G. H.

TANNER, W.
TAYLOR, C.
TAYLOR, F. H.
TAYLOR, J. B.
TAYLOR, R. G.
TAYLOR, W.
TERRY, T. W.
THEOBALD, E. W.
THOMAS, J. P.
THORNE, R. H.
THORP, A. E.
TOMS, M. R.
TOWILL, W. A.
TOZER, R. G.
TRESIZE, G. S.
TREVASSA, L. W. C.
TUCKER, J. H.
TUCKER, P.
TURK, C.
TURNER, G.
TYERS, K. G.

UNDERHAY, W. G.

VALE, H.
VALLANCE, W. J.
VANNECK, R. W.
VANSCOLINA, F. W.
VICKERY, M. A.

WADLANG, F.
WALKER, C. J.
WALLIS, A. J.
WALLIS, F. E.
WALLIS, F. R.
WARD, C. H.
WARDEN, A. R. A.
WATSON, R. A.
WEATHERHEAD, E. S.
WEBB, J. H.
WEBBER, E. J.
WEBBER, S. G.
WEBSTER, J. C.
WELCH, J.
WELCH, J. P.
WELCH, L. N.
WELLINGTON, F.
WELTON, W. K.
WESTACOTT, L.
WESTAWAY, A.
WHEADON, H. S.
WHERRY, K. L.
WHITAKER, W. J.
WHITE, C. A.
WHITE, F. J.
WHITE, J. F.
WIDDICOMBE, W.
WILKINSON, C. B.
WILLIAMS, A.
WILLIAMS, E. H.
WILLIAMSON, S. E.
WILLS, A. J. R.
WILLS, S. G.
WILSON, J. P.
WILSON, R. B.
WINSOR, F.
WONNACOTT, W. J.
WOOD, E. H.
WOOD, J. C.
WORTH, L.
WOTTON, F. H.
WOTTON, M.
WRIGHT, G.
WYATT, L. J.
WYATT, T. C. S.

"H" COMPANY

Lt.-Colonel
DAVIES, R. D.

Majors
COLERIDGE, P. L., O.B.E.
JAMES, R. G.
KENNEDY, R., D.S.O., M.C.
KNOLLYS, A. G., M.C.

Captain and Adjutant
MARCH, F. J.

Lieutenants
COOMBES, A. L.

CROOK, L. J.
EVERSLEY-GREEN, A. N.
HEDELIUS, McW.
SMITH, A. J.

2nd Lieutenants
BRAUND, J. O.
LINSCOTT, E. J. C.

Warrant Officers
GEORGE, F. M., D.C.M.
LANGLEY-ELLIS, G. A.
NEWTON, W. A. H.
REED, H. E.

Colour Sergeant
MacPHERSON, K.

Sergeants
ANDREWS, H. E. J.
BIRD, D. W. C.
CALLARD, B.
COLE, W. C.
KELLOW, J., M.M.
KELLY, D. W.
KNEIL, C. H.
LONGTHORPE, S. R.
MINNS, W. W. C.
MITCHELL, D. R.
NORTHWAY, R. H. J.

"H" COMPANY—continued

REEVES, S. H.
SATTERLEY, F. R.
STILLIARD, F. P.
WENBORN, E. N.
WILLIAMS, S. E.
WILSON, E. J. M.
WOLFF, W. E.

Corporals and Bombardiers
ABRAHAM, H. C.
ALLRIGHT, P.
CROCKER, C. R.
EASTERBROOK, R. S.
EGGBEER, R. J.
EVANS, G. L.
FITZGERALD, J. D.
FORD, C. H.
GEORGE, L. R.
HALL, A. T.
HARRIS, J.
JOHNS, F.
LEVETT, H. C.
MARTIN, G. E.
ROYLE, E.
SHORT, K. G.
SKELTON, H. R.
TRAYHURN, W. G.

L/Corporals & L/Bombardiers
AVERY, E. G.
BALMENT, F. J.
BARKER, K. A.
BROOKMAN, D. J.
DOWN, J. H.
EDGECOMBE, R. F.
ENDACOTT, L. T.
FIELD, G. E.
FORD, J.
GATTING, H. R.
GILL, W. T.
HANNAFORD, W. A.
HARVEY, H.
HAYNES, R. G.
HOWLETT, A. P.
JOHN, G.
OLDFIELD, L.
PAGE, A. H.
PALFREY, W. F.
PALK, H. G.
PHILLIPS, J.
PRICE, A. W.
RANDELL, A. V.
SARAHS, H. W.
SHERWELL, W. G.
STEVENS, A. E. J.
WARD, E. L.
WELLINGTON, F. G.
WHITEHORN, C. F.

Privates and Gunners
ABSOLON, N. H.
ADCOCK, G. E.
ALFORD, F. W.
ALLEN, F. W. N.
ALLEN, P. L.
ALLEN, W. C.
ALLEN, W. J. P.
ALLERY, G.
ALLISON, E. W.
ALLWOOD, W. T.
ALMOND, J. S.
ANDREWS, W. F. J.
AVERY, F. A.
AVERY, P.
ARGYLE, E.
ASHBY, R. C. E.
ASHPLANT, B. F. H.

ASHTON, C. R
AUSTIN, A. G.
AUSTIN, W. T. F.
BAILEY, R. G. H.
BAKER, J.
BAKER, F. W.
BAKER, H. C.
BAKER, R. V.
BALKWILL, E.
BANCROFT, R. F.
BANCROFT, S. P.
BANFIELD, V.
BANNISTER, P. J.
BARLOW, R.
BARRETT, E. S.
BARTER, J.
BARTLETT, J. H.
BARTLETT, L. S.
BARTLETT, T.
BASS, W. H.
BATTISON, R. C.
BAWDEN, P. A.
BAXTER, W.
BEARD, G. A.
BEARMAN, W.
BEARNE, F.
BEARNS, A.
BEDFORD, A.
BELLAMY, R. J.
BALLAMY, C. J.
BELL, W. H.
BENNETT, S. A.
BENSON, J. E.
BEST, E. R.
BICKLEY, J. G.
BLACKLER, L. S.
BLACKMORE, R. A. J.
BLATCHFORD, D. A.
BLIGHT, L. T. L.
BOLT, R. C.
BOND, J. E. G.
BOOTH, A. J.
BOUGET, C. B.
BOWDEN, W. J.
BOYD, J.
BOYD, S.
BRADBURY, G. F. J.
BRADFORD, A. E.
BRANDRETH, W. E.
BRAY, R. A. H.
BRIGHT, B. C.
BRIGHT, L. R.
BRILL, C. E.
BRIMILCOMBE, L. G.
BRISTOW, T. G.
BRITT, G.
BROOM, R. H.
BROWN, F. J.
BROWN, G.
BROWN, J. H.
BROWN, R.
BROWN, R. E.
BRUCE, S. H.
BRYANT, F.
BUCK, R. J.
BUCKINGHAM, G. J.
BUCKPITT, J. T.
BUCKPITT, W. J.
BUNKER, W. H.
BUNNY, E. J.
BURDEN, G. W.
BURGOYNE, F. E.
BUSCOMBE, H. C.
BUTT, F. A.
BUTTIFANT, S. H.

CAMPBELL, A. A.

CARRUTHERS, P. J.
CARTER, L. C. J.
CHAFFE, J. L.
CHALK, C. A.
CHALK, G. J..
CHALKER, R. A. J.
CHALLICE, A.
CHAPMAN, S. C.
CHARD, E. W.
CHESTERFIELD, H. R. J.
CHUBB, L. F.
CHUBB, N. J. P.
CHUDLEY, A. E.
CLARK, B. W. N. I.
CLARK, M. R.
CLARK, W.
CLARK, W. R.
CLEMENTS, W. T.
CODY, H. E. B.
COE, N. E.
COLE, W. C.
COLEMAN, W. J.
COLES, A. W.
COLLINGS, A. R.
COLLINGS, J. A.
COLSON, A.
COLWILL, G. H.
COMPTON, G.
COOK, G. S.
COOPER, K. E.
COOPER, W. J. T.
CORNER, H. C.
COX, K. V.
COYDE, F. G.
CRANFIELD, V. E. A.
CRISPIN, G. T.
CROCKER, W. H. C.
CROOKSHANK, C. K.
CROSBIE, H. B.

DADSWELL, S. J.
DAGWORTHY, R. A.
DAMEREL, A. S.
DANN, A. T.
DAVEY, A. H.
DAVID, G.
DAVIES, E.
DAVIES, E. T.
DAVIES, K. R.
DAWE, W. H.
DEBENHAM, H. J. N.
DENBOW, F.
DENTUS, S.
DEWARDT, S.
DIBDEN, C. A.
DICKER, W. J.
DIMOND, F.
DODD, J. C.
DOLLEY, A. W. J.
DONABIE, E. R. P.
DONEY, L.
DONEY, L. C.
DOWN, R. J.
DOWNING, P. J.
DROMEY, T. J.
DURBIN, E. G.
DUNN, W. H.
DWYER, W. P.
DYER, C. W.
DYKE, H. J.

EAD, E. R.
EAD, P. M.
EAKERS, C. J.
EARL, F. P.
EATON, N. P.
EDMONDS, A. W.

"H" COMPANY—continued

EDMONDS, W. P.
EDWARDS, B. F. H.
EFFER, R. P.
ELLIS, J. G. R.
ELLIS, W. R.
ENGLAND, E. B.
EVANS, J. D.
EVANS, J.
EVANS, R. F.
EVERITT, S. O.

FAIREY, C. W. F.
FARRANT, G. G.
FARTHING, H. E. R.
FAULKNER, E. F.
FERENS, J. J. T.
FERRIS, E. N.
FIELD, S. E.
FILKINS, W. G.
FINCH, N. P.
FISHER, P. J.
FISHWICK, J. H.
FLETCHER, H.
FORD, W. A.
FORD, D. L.
FOULKES, A.
FOX, N. W.
FRASER, D. M.
FRENCH, H. S.
FROST, W.
FRY, H. J.
FULL, E. E.

GALE, C. E.
GALE, K. E.
GARDNER, D. A.
GATTING, F. J.
GEORGE, A. E.
GEORGE, F. T.
GIBBARD, H.
GIBBS, P. H. L.
GIFFORD, A. H.
GILES, B. P.
GILLARD, S. T.
GODFREY, K. F.
GOLDSWORTHY, C. E.
GOODHEART, C. H.
GOODING, E. T.
GOODMAN, H. A.
GOSS, C. L.
GOSS, K. A. J.
GOUGH, E. J. S.
GOVE, W. G.
GOWMAN, W. J.
GRAY, P. J. S.
GREEN, K.
GREENER, N. B.
GRIFFITHS, A. W.

HALLETT, L. P.
HALY, R. J.
HAM, W. E.
HANCOCK, E. J.
HANCOCK, H. R.
HANNAFORD, E. J.
HANNAFORD, F. E.
HANNAFORD, H. E.
HARDING, A. K.
HARDING, P. R.
HARRIS, A. J.
HARRIS, J. W.
HARRIS, P. J.
HARRISON, D. J.
HARRY, L.
HART, A. J. F.
HART, R. J. T.
HARVERSON, C. A.

HARVEY, R. G.
HARVEY, S. F.
HARVEY, W. H.
HASLAM, J. G.
HASLAM, R.
HATHERLEY, E. T.
HATHERLEY, W. R.
HAWKE, W. H.
HAWKINS, L. J.
HAWKINS, R. F.
HAYMAN, J.
HAYTER, F. G.
HEAD, L. M.
HEAD, R. G. C.
HEAL, F. J.
HEARN, W. J.
HEATH, L. N.
HEATH, L. F.
HEATH, N. F.
HEATH, P. S.
HENSON, J.
HELE, R. S. J.
HEPBURN, K.
HESKETH, F. H.
HIBBERD, D. N.
HICKS, C.
HIGGINS, A. H.
HIGGS, R.
HILL, R. T.
HILL, W. E.
HIND, A. F.
HINE, H. S.
HOBBS, S. G. J.
HODGE, F.
HOGDON, T.
HOLLYER, C. J.
HOLMAN, C. E.
HOLMAN, K. W.
HONEYWILL, F. G.
HOOKWAY, S. A.
HORLER, C. M.
HORN, L. C.
HORTON, R.
HOSKIN, B.
HOSKIN, J.
HOUGHTON, W. G.
HOWARD, R. M.
HOWARD, W. H.
HUGHES, C. M.
HUMPHREYS, R. W.
HUMPHREYS-DAVIES, G. A.
HUNT, C. W.
HUNT, F. J.
HUNT, R. W. J.
HUTCHINGS, P.
HUTCHINGS, A. H.

IDE, D.
INKPEN, F. G.

JAGO, A.
JAMES, T. C.
JARVIS, E. J.
JASPER, L. V.
JEFFERY, W. H.
JENKIN, A. L.
JENKINS, D. H.
JENKINS, W. F.
JEWELL, R. T. J.
JOHNSTONE, R. E.
JONES, C. N.
JONES, E.
JONES, E. A.
JONES, J.
JONES, R. D.
JONES, R.

JOY, G.
JOY, J. E.

KEENE, C. M.
KEENOR, A. G.
KERSWELL, F. C. T.
KING, A. J.
KINCH, W. S.
KNAPMAN, C. F.
KNIVETON, R. W.

LAMB, W. J.
LANDER, J. E.
LANG, C. G. H.
LANG, T.
LANDSELL, F. C.
LAVIS, W. J.
LAYFIELD, R.
LEDGER, W. J.
LEE, E. A.
LEE, E. A.
LEGGE, B. G.
LE MARE, L.
LEY, F. E.
LEY, L. G.
LIDDLE, S.
LOCKYER, C. E.
LONGLEY-COOK, L. H.
LOVEYS, V. A.
LOW, J. F.
LOWE, J. J.
LOWE, W. G.
LOWRY, G. L. B.
LUGGER, W. H.
LUKE, R. E.
LUSCOMBE, G. H.
LUXTON, C. W. B.

McALPINE, R.
McCABE, E.
McMAHON, P. R.
McNAUGHTON, T. D.
MADGE, C. J. A.
MADGE, W. H.
MALTBY, J. H.
MARCH, W. L.
MARSH, C. H.
MARSHALL, E. J. L.
MARTIN, F. C.
MARTIN, R. L. H.
MARTIN, R. S.
MARTIN, R. W.
MARTIN, S. T.
MARTIN, T.
MARTIN, W. H.
MARTYN, G.
MAY, K.
MAYDWELL, W. D.
MEAKIN, W. J.
MELLOR, A.
MEMBERY, W. G.
MERCER, O. C.
MERRIFIELD, R. J.
MILES, H. R.
MILLEDGE, E. D.
MILLER, T. E.
MILLINGTON, R. H.
MILLS, G. E.
MILLS, S. J.
MILLWARD, E. R.
MINSHIP, L.
MITCHELL, J. G.
MOORE, S. A.
MORECOMBE, J. A.
MORGAN, H. W.
MORRIS, A. G.
MORRIS, G. H.

"H" COMPANY—continued

MORRISON, C. F.
MOULTON, S. J. T.
MOXHAY, D. W.
MOXHAY, E. F.
MULLEN, E. L.
MUNSON, R. W.
MURPHY, N. S.

NEALE, C. F.
NETHERWAY, P. T.
NEWBAND, R.
NEWBERRY, W. G. W.
NEWBURY, S. G.
NEWCOMBE, J. P.
NICHOLAS, J. R.
NICHOLLS, F. L. A.
NICHOLLS, F. W.
NICHOL, H. H.
NICHOLSON, R. R. A.
NICHOLSON, L. R.
NICKELS, A. F. G.
NORRIS, E. G.
NORRIS, W. J.
NORTHCOTT, W. P.
NORTHWAY, C. T.
NORTHWAY, R. R.
NUNNEY, G. W.
NUTTALL, W.

OAKLEY, F. D.
OLDS, C.
OLVER, F. J.
OSBORNE, J. C.
OWEN, D. G.

PALMER, N. V.
PARKER, F.
PARKER, W. D. G.
PARKMAN, L.
PARSONS, G.
PARSONS, J. L.
PASSMORE, D.
PATEMAN, L. E.
PEARCE, F. G.
PEARCE, G. E.
PEARN, A. R.
PEDLER, S. W.
PELLY, C. A.
PENWILL, R. E.
PENWILL, R. J.
PENWILL, S. C.
PERCY, C. W. H.
PERRETT, R. B.
PERRIN, R.
PERRING, G. C.
PERRY, F. E.
PERRY, F. J.
PETHERICK, A. E.
PETHERICK, J.
PHEAR, H.
PHILP, W.
PHILLIPS, P.
PICTON, J. F.
PIKE, C. A.
PIKE, G. C.
PILLAGE, J. R.
PIPPIN, W.
PLATT, R. E.
PLUMB, W. A.
POLLARD, W. H.
POLLARD, W. E. R.
POLYBLANK, T. G.
PONTING, G.
POPE, R. H.
POPMAN, M. G.
PORT, F.
PORTER, R. C.

POTHAM, E. P.
POWELL, H. C.
PRESCOTT, P. W.
PRICE, A.
PROCTOR, D. B. V.
PROSSER, R. C.
PROWSE, C. C.
PROWSE, R. G.
PUGSLEY, H. A.
PULHAM, R. J.
PURDY, G. N.
PYNE, R. M.

QUICK, S. J.

RAE-SMITH, C.
RANDALL, D.
RAWLING, W. C.
RAYMOND, G. R.
READ, P. H.
READ, R. W.
REDFERN, L. F.
REED, G. C.
REEVE, D. G. W.
REEVES, W. C. L.
RENDELL, F.
RENDLE, J. T.
RICE, G. A.
RIDLEY, L.
ROBERTS, A. W.
ROBERTS, F. J.
ROBERTS, H.
ROBERTS, W. H.
ROBINS, J. H. L.
ROBINSON, A. J.
ROBSON, A.
ROBYNS, J. T.
ROCHESTER, R. N.
ROCKETT, J. T.
ROGERS, S. D.
ROOK, E. R.
ROOK, G. S.
ROOST, H. C.
ROPER, W. E. G.
ROSENHEIM, S. S.
ROWE, C. M.
ROWLANDS, P. J.
ROWLEY, K. G.
RUGGLES, R. J.
RUNDLE, A. V. G.
RUSSELL, M. F.

SAGE, S. J.
SAMPSON, L. J.
SARAHS, R. C.
SATTERLEY, M. E.
SATTERLEY, W. A.
SAUNDERS, H. T.
SAUNDERS, R. A. J. W.
SAVAGE, T. G.
SCAFELL, R. J.
SCAIFE, V. C.
SCANES, H. J.
SCREECH, G. C.
SEARLE, T. H.
SEARLE, W. J.
SELWAY, H. McD.
SERCOMBE, G.
SHARP, V. D.
SHERRELL, L. J.
SHOBROOK, L.
SHOBROOK, T.
SHORT, P. J.
SHORT, W. J.
SIMPSON, J. V.
SIMPSON, R. P.
SKEDGEL, H. J.

SKINNER, D. A.
SKINNER, W. F. M.
SMALE, B. J.
SMALE, H. R.
SMITH, G.
SMITH, R. J. S.
SMITH, L. G.
SMITH, S. J.
SMITH, W.
SMYTH, G. S. A.
SOMERVILLE, W. G.
SOUTHWOOD, W. H.
SPARSHOTT, R.
SPILLER, W. J.
STANNETT, A. J.
STAPLETON, W. G.
STEER, G. H.
STEPHENS, C.
STEVENS, F. W.
STEVENS, O. G.
STONE, J. H.
STRANGER, R.
STREET, E. E.
STUCKEY, T. H.
SUTCHELL, F. F.
SUTCLIFFE, W.
SWEETLAND, H.
SYMONS, E. S.

TANNER, B. M.
TAPLEY, A.
TARREN, T. W.
TAYLOR, R. J. R.
TAYLOR, S.
TAYLOR, W. H.
THEAKER, H.
THOMAS, H. R.
THOMAS, R. G.
THOMPSON, H. H.
THOMPSON, R.
THOMPSON, G. H. S.
THORNE, B. J.
THURNELL, J. H.
TIBBS, J.
TILEY, J. W. T.
TILL, L. H. A.
TILLBROOK, P. H. G.
TIMSON, A.
TIPPER, P.
TOBIN, J.
TOLCHARD, A. R.
TOMS, R. G. J.
TONKYN, F. M.
TORRY, G. C.
TOWNSEND, T.
TOZER, N. R.
TREACHER, R. H.
TREBY, R.
TREDGETT, J. H.
TREDINNICK, G. H. F.
TROUT, J. W.
TUCKER, G.
TUCKER, M. W.
TURNER, S. G.
TWOMEY, J. J.

VEALE, N. E.
VELVICK, A. E.
VELVICK, C. J.
VENTON, R.
VINE, R.

WALLACE, S. A. B.
WARREN, C. W.
WATSON, C. N.
WATSON, D. M.
WATERSON, W. J.

"H" COMPANY—continued

WATT, P. N.
WAY, W. F. B.
WAYMOUTH, C. J.
WEBBER, V. J.
WEBSTER, R. M.
WEDDEN, W. H.
WEEKS, A. E. J.
WEEKS, C. N. J.
WEEKS, G. A.
WEEKES, S. J.
WEISS, C. R.
WELLS, L. E.
WESTACOTT, J. H.
WESTAWAY, R. G.
WESTCOTT, A. E.
WESTLAKE, A. W.
WESTLAKE, E. G.
WHARHIRST, F.
WHEAR, G. L. D.
WHETTER, C. W.
WHITE, J. W.
WHITE, P. G. A.

WHITE, W.
WHITEHOUSE, T. G.
WILDE, E. J.
WILLCOCKS, S. F.
WILLIAMS, B. H.
WILLIAMS, C. V.
WILLIAMS, C. W. S.
WILLIAMS, E. H.
WILLIAMS, F. E.
WILLIAMS, N.
WILLIAMS, R. J.
WILLIAMS, T.
WILLIAMS, T. J.
WILLIAMS, W. H.
WILLS, H. A.
WILLS, W. E.
WILSON, C.
WILSON, D. H.
WINDEATT, A. B.
WINSOR, S. L.
WINTLE, P. H.
WISEMAN, A.

WISHART, J. C.
WOOD, A. W.
WOOD, L. T.
WOODMAN, J. T. B.
WOODROW, S. W.
WORDEN, C. D.
WORRALL, L. A.
WORRALL, L. J.
WOTTON, V. W.
WOTTON, W. J.
WOTTON, W.
WRIGHT, W. J. G.
WYATT, R. H.

YELDHAM, K. N.
YELLAND, A. J.
YOULDEN, F. J.
YOUNG, I. D.
YOUNG, M. C.

ZAPLE, R. G.

PRESENT MEMBERS
as at December, 1944

Lists compiled from
Part III Orders

"A" COMPANY

Major
EGGBEER, R. J.

Captains
BENNETT, F. J.
WARREN, J. F.

Lieutenants
CROSSMAN, C. H.
ELLIS, C. F.
FRAYN, R.
HOOPER, S. E.
JEFFERY, E. A.
LEWIS, H. S.
VALLANCE, F. J.
WARD, C. H. G.
WILLIAMS, F. G. V.

2nd Lieutenants
McMORRAN, N. G.
RAIKES, J. W. J.

C.S.M.
MAYFIELD, W. E.

C.Q.M.S.
EVERDELL, F. C.

Sergeants
ANDREWS, G. E.
BENDLE, W. S.
BIDDICK, H. J. C.
BURT, E. F.
BURTON, E.
COAST, H. J.
DAVEY, C.
FERGUSON, M.
GODBEER, C. E.
HIDER, E. J.
LUTON, R. P.
MARTIN, W.
MOHAN, H. A.
NICKELS, C. D.
PALMER, R. H.
PLYMSOL, E. W.
POOLEY, W. G.
RANDALL, H. J.
SEAMAN, G. W.
SPEARE, J.
STADDON, M. R.
VICKERY, W. N.
WADHAM, P. W.
WRENN, F. H.

Corporals
BAKER, T.
BEARNE, W. E.
BICKNELL, W. A.
BURN, C. H.
COLE, A.
COYSH, C. T.
CRABB, J.
DAVEY, H. G.
EASTERBROOK, H. W.
ELSTON, A. D.
GEORGE, P. R.
GOODYEAR, C.
GREEN, W. T.
HARWOOD, P. A.
HAYWOOD, E. R.
JERMAN, F. S.
JOHN, C.
MOORE, F. H.
NORRIS, W. F.
NORRISH, A. R.

QUARTLY, S. F.
ROBINSON, F. W.
ROWLEY, F. H. J.
SHAKESPEARE, A. E.
SIMS, C.
SMITH, D. L.
SOWDEN, H.
SRODZINSKI, R. A. G.
STANDOMBE, R.
WARREN, P. M.
WENSLEY, A. F.
WOOD, W.

Lance Corporals
BEER, C. M.
CHESTERMAN, R.
COLES, R.
COOKSLEY, R. J.
COX, F.
ELLIS, O. P. P.
GIBBINGS, G. H.
GOLLIDGE, P. N.
HEMMINGS, F.
HIBBS, F. C.
HUNT, R. G.
LOW, H. G.
NICHOLAS, S. H.
PATEMAN, R. J.
PERRING, J. J.
PLYMSOL, F. S.
SADLER, G. E.
SANDERS, W. J.
SHARLAND, A. W.
SHORT, H. J.
STAINES, F. A.
STOCKMAN, J. W.
WADSWORTH, W.
WILLIAMS, L., D.C.M.
WYATT, J. H.

Privates
ACTON, A. H.
ADAMS, A. E.
ADDISON, G. E.
ALLEN, F.
ANDREWS, C. H.
ANNING, C.
ANTILL, W. H.
APLIN, B.
ASH, E.
ASH, W. W.
ATTWOOD, G.
AUGER, J. W.
AYRES, T. E.
BACKHOLER, W. C.
BAKER, G. E.
BAKER, W J.
BAKER, G. T.
BALMENT, F. J.
BANNISTER, A. C.
BARKER, H. V.
BASTOW, W.
BEDDALL, F. J.
BEER, P. W.
BELL, N. G.
BENNETT, G.
BEYNON, F. H.
BICKNELL, H. C.
BIRD, H. F.
BLACKMORE, R. A.
BLACKMORE, R. R.
BLATCHFORD, L. W.
BOVEY, F.
BOWDEN, A. A.

BOWDEN, E. A.
BOWDEN, R. W.
BREALY, R. W.
BROADBRIDGE, W. G.
BROADHURST, E. E.
BROOK, C. S.
BUDD, P. J.
BULLEY, A.
BULLOCK, A. H.
BURT, E. R. G.

CAFFRY, A. R.
CALLICOTT, A.
CAMP, J. W.
CAMP, W. D.
CARD, E. P.
CAUSEY, H. W. B.
CHEAL, J. H.
CHERRY, F. B. C.
CLEGG, S. W. J.
CLEMENTS, A. E.
CLEMENTS, A. J.
CLOKE, C.
COLE, W. L.
COLES, J.
COWLING, E. S.
COX, E. M.
CRABBE, G. P.
CRISPIN, W. S.

DARKE, T. F.
DAVEY, E. T.
DAVEY, E. V.
DAVEY, W. H.
DAVIES, E.
DAVIES, W. M.
DAVIS, G. O.
DITTON, E. R. J.
DREW, A. J.

EALES, E. P.
EDWARDS, C. E.
ELLIS, G. D.
EVANS, P.
EXELL, H. E.

FINCH, R. H.
FRANKS, C. J.
FRANKS, H. B.
FRAYN, J.
FRENCH, H. J.
FRENCH, J. T.

GEORGE, J.
GIBBINGS, S.
GILES, G. G.
GILL, C. S. M.
GRIMES, T.
GROVER, H. T. R. N.

HALLIDAY, R.
HAMMETT, G.
HAMMOND, J. F.
HANNAFORD, G. H.
HARDY, G.
HARLEY, F. E. L.
HARLEY, R.
HARVEY, F. W. H.
HARVEY, H. T.
HASLER, H. G.
HATHERLEY, S.
HAWKEN, G. R.
HAWKINS, B.
HAYDEN, R. J.
HEAD, R. J.

"A" COMPANY—continued

HEALE, A. R.
HEALE, H. J.
HEBBES, F. N.
HELYAR, D. W.
HERD, A. G.
HIGGINS, O. T.
HILL, H. M.
HILL, W. E.
HOAR, A. H.
HOARE, H. G.
HOARD, W. F.
HOCKRIDGE, S. T.
HOLLAND, A. E.
HOLLOWAY, A. H.
HOLMAN, R. S. E.
HOLWILL, H.
HORSWELL, A. C.
HORTON, R.
HUNDLEY, J. M.
HUNT, H. J.
HUNTER, S. H.
HYNE, M. F. J.

INGRAM, F. B.
ISAAC, G. T.
ISAAC, J. W. H.

JAMES, H. C.
JEFFERY, J. A.
JORDAN, C. T. J.

KEEN, P. G.
KEOGH, J. N.
KING, T. E.
KIRKBY, C. E.
KNAPMAN, E. H.
KNOWLES, G. W.

LANE, E. A. G.
LANGDON, J. C.
LANGMEAD, W. F. T.
LAROCHE, H. L. E.
LAW, L.
LEONARD, A. V.
LODER, S. H.
LORD, F. G.

MADAN, A. G.
MADGE, C. H.
MADGE, W. H.
MANN, E. W.
MARCHANT, W.
MARLES, R. J.
MARLOW, F.
MATHEWS, A. T.
MEEK, W. F.
MILES, G.
MILLER, L. G.
MILLS, W. A. E.

MITCHELL, B. C.
MORGAN, F. R.
MORTIMORE, D. A.

NICHOLLS, F. J.
NORRISH, F. P.
NORTHWAY, R. R.

OATWAY, L.
O'KEEFFE, T.
OLDING, F. G.
OSBORNE, A. W.

PALMER, G. C.
PARNELL, A. E.
PARNELL, H. B.
PAYNE, F.
PAYNE, S.
PEARCE, C. H.
PENGELLY, A. E.
PENWARDEN, W. J.
PERRING, W. J. L.
PHILLIPPOT, J. A.
PICKARD, L. R.
PIKE, F. J.
PIKE, R. J.
PINNEY, A. J.
PLEACE, E. H.
POOK, E. S.
POPE, E. J.
PRICE, A.
PROWSE, C. A.
PUGH, A. E. E.
PUTT, D. A.

RAPSON, A. H.
RAY, A. H.
RAY, C. H.
RIMMER, T.
RING, D.
ROBERTS, G. F.
ROBINSON, C. C.
ROBINSON, J. W.
ROWE, C. E.
ROWE, W. F.

SANDERS, B. H.
SANDS, A. R.
SAUNDERS, E. R
SCOTT, W. J.
SCREECH, C. W. J.
SERCOMBE, W. T. A.
SHEPHARD, G. H.
SHORLAND, C.
SLOCOMBE, A. H.
SLOMAN, F.
SLUGGETT, H.
SLUGGETT, W.

SMALE, A. T.
SMALE, H. R.
SMITH, C.
SMITH, W. C.
SOUTHWOOD, H. J.
STAMP, J. A.
STANBURY, S. J.
STEVENS, F. G.
STEVENS, S. J.
STICKLAND, R. J.
STOCKER, W. D.
STOCKMAN, A. S.
STOCKMAN, S. H.
STOCKWELL, H. C.
STUCKEY, S.

TANDY, H. V.
TANDY, T.
TEARLE, J. H.
TOZER, E. V.
TOZER, N. R.
TOZER, W. L.
TROWT, W. J.
TUCK, H. N.
TWEEDY, G. H.

VACHELL, E. T.
VEYSEY, F. F.
VINCENT, E. G.
VINCENT, F.
VOWDEN, J. W.

WAKEHAM, W. E. N.
WALKER, A. W.
WALTON, C. G.
WALTON, G. W.
WARD, A. P.
WARD, K. P.
WARNE, A.
WATKINS, W. T. C.
WATSON, H.
WATTS, C.
WEEKS, H. E.
WEEKS, W. A.
WELLINGTON, W. P.
WESTCOTT, A. E.
WESTERN, G. A.
WHITE, F.
WHITE, S. G.
WIDDICOMBE, T. A.
WILLIAMS, L., D.C.M.
WILLS, F.
WINDEATT, R. B.
WITTEN, R.
WOOD, H.
WOODERS, F. W.
WOODMORE, J.
WRIGHT, S. D.

"B" COMPANY

Major
WILLIAMS, R. P.

Captains
WADE, P., R.A.M.C.
WELLMAN, R. R.

Lieutenants
ADAMS, H. W.
BROWN, A. E. O., M.C.
DAMPIER, C. R.
JONES, D. R. G.
LESLEY, O. C. B.

LIDSTONE, G. H.
MATTHEWS, G. W.
WILSON, B. T.

2nd Lieutenants
HANNAFORD, E. J.
PATEMAN, M. W. L.

C.S.M.
HALAHAN, A. C., O.B.E.

C.Q.M.S.
BRADY, J., M.S.M.

Sergeants
BRADFORD, W. F., M.M.
BRAGG, H. P.
CURTIS, P. J., M.S.M.
DALE, W. C.
EALES, R. H.
EDWARDS, A. J.
FENNELL, W. A.
GUTSELL, W. C.
HAWKINS, E.
HOLLYER, H. B., M.M.
MILLER, W. B.
PHILLIPS, F. A.

"B" COMPANY—continued

RIDER, A. E.
SEARLE, F. E.
SEYMOUR, A. W., C.M.G.
SPARKES, J.
TAPLEY, E. G.
TUCKER, W. F.
WARD, H. F.
WESTAWAY, T. F.
WOODHALL, H. W.

A/Sergeants
IVEY, J. R.
TOMLIN, C. J.

Corporals
ABBS, F. H.
ANNING, C. L.
ANNING, F. J.
BABBAGE, C. E.
BRANCH, W. J.
BRINHAM, S.
CHALK, F. W.
COLES, H. A. T.
COONEY, D. A.
DOBSON, F. C.
ELLIS, O. R.
FOSTER, S. R.
FRAYNE, A.
GARDNER, V. R. G.
GUEST, L. I.
HAYWARD, R. J.
HEAD, N. A.
HILL, J. A.
HOLLINS, E.
HOWKINS, J. D.
JEFFERIES, C. H.
KERNICK, R. S.
LEAMAN, A.
LEEMAN, J. A.
LOUNT, A. H.
MANLEY, E.
MANLEY, H. E.
MARKHAM, A.
MATTHEWS, B. C.
MAY, J. W. E.
MORGAN, B. J.
NEAL, C. B.
NICHOLSON, J. A.
NOYES, T.
POWELL, J.
SARGEANT, E. J.
SAUNDERS, F. F.
SHARPE, B. A.
SOMERVILLE, J. E.
SPLATT, F. W.
STONE, G. A.
THOMAS, E. V.
WALTERS, L. E.
WALTON, C. H.
WESTBROOK, P. B.
WHATLEY, C. R.
WILLIAMS, A. H.
WILLS, T. H.

Lance Corporals
BAXTER, W. W.
BISHOP, J. J.
BLACKMORE, H. S.
BUCKLEY, K. W.
BUSWELL, E. F.
CATER, J.
CLARKE, J.
CONNAUGHTON, A.
CROCKER, A. J. B.
DAMERELL, A. H.
DARKE, A. V.

DUDMAN, W.
FRANKLIN, T. H.
FURNEAUX, T.
FURSDON, R. J.
GARLAND, J. O.
HEATH, H.
HUTCHINGS, C. T.
LORAM, F. H.
MARTIN, P.
MILLER, H. E.
OLDREY, E. W. H.
PAXTON, P. J.
PITTS, F. G.
POULTER, W. J.
ROBINS, H. G. S.
RODGERS, A. H.
SANDERS, E. F. K.
SCOTT, J. B.
SHAPLEY, J. C.
SPLATT, E. J.
VALLIS, G. A.
WANNELL, L. J.
WAY, J. R.
WHITE, B. R.
WILLIAMS, A. W.

Privates
ADAMS, E. W. G.
ADAMS, R. J.
ADDEMS, W. C.
ALLEN, G. A.
ARTHUR, W. S.
AVERY, W. R. H.

BABER, H. R. J.
BAKER, A. J.
BAKER, L. C. R.
BALL, J. J.
BALSDON, H. F.
BARNETT, M. H.
BARRAND, W.
BARRETT, A. J.
BARTLETT, W. H.
BARTLEY, J.
BASTOW, R. A.
BATTERSHILL, H.
BENJAMIN, P. J.
BEWHAY, W. C.
BISH, H. E.
BLACKLER, K. E.
BLACKLER, S. E.
BLACKSHAW, F. W.
BOLE, W. R.
BOLLAND, H. T.
BOLT, W. E.
BOTT, W. G.
BOVEY, C. C. H.
BOWDEN, E. A.
BOWDEN, E. H.
BOWHAY, H. L.
BRAUN, J. T.
BRISTOW, R. J.
BROKENSHIRE, H.
BROOKING, P. J.
BROWN, A. H.
BROWN, H.
BROWN, H. A.
BROWN, F. J.
BROWN, F. O.
BROWNING, G.
BUDD, C. A.
BULLEN, F. H.
BUNCH, A. H.
BUTTLE, W.

CANN, A.

CANN, S.
CHAMBERS, G. J.
CHAPMAN, J. H. A.
CHEESEWORTH, E. L.
CLEMENTS, P. W.
CLIFFORD, P. J.
COKER, C. J.
COLE, H.
COLEMAN, A. H.
CORNISH, J.
COWELL, S. C. W.
COX, A. H. R.
COX, A. J.
COX, D. E.
CRAYTON, A. G.
CREWS, W. J.
CROUCH, J.
CURTIS, E.

DARE, S.
DARKE, H. F.
DAVEY, L.
DISNEY, S. G.
DOBLE, D.
DODD, B.
DOMMETT, F. M.
DOWNEY, J. W.
DRAKE, F. A.
DRAKE, F. H. L.
DREW, F. W.

EDEN, B. W.
EDEN, L. H.
EDEN, S. C.
ELLIS, A. H.
ELSON, S. E.
ELSTON, W. E.
ENDACOTT, R. A.

FAIRS, J. A.
FARLEY, W. F. J.
FAWCETT, J. W.
FEGAN, J. R.
FERGUSON, A.
FINN, J. T. C.
FLEET, A. J.
FLORY, F. E.
FORWILL, C. H.
FRAPWELL, E.
FRIEND, L. J.
FURNEAUX, J. E.

GALOWITZ, A.
GARNER, J.
GAY, F. J. J.
GIBBINGS, J. E.
GIBSON, W.
GILL, A. S.
GRAHAM, W. A.
GREENSLADE, A.
GRIFFIN, W. G.
GUEST, G. D.

HAJITTOULI, M. K.
HAMMOND, R. J. A.
HANCOCK, E. J. J. V. P.
HANSFORD, N. G.
HARRIS, J. G.
HARRIS, K. W.
HARVEY, F. T.
HASLAM, C. F.
HAYMAN, A. C. V.
HAYMAN, R. S.
HEATH, W. A. E.
HELLIER, C. A.
HENSON, R. R.

"B" COMPANY—continued

HINGSTON, D. W.
HOLLIDAY, F. H.
HOLMAN, P. J.
HOLTHAM, P. J.
HOOPER, J. H.
HOOPER, W. C.
HORSHAM, S. A. J.
HOWE, R. L.
HUGHES, G. R.
HUTCHINGS, W. G.

IREDALE, F. H.
ISAAC, W. H.

JACKSON, I. D.
JANES, W. H.
JELLEY, L. F. G.
JENKINS, E. W.
JONES, K. W.
JORDAN, F.

KEARVELL, R. W.
KELLAND, T.
KEMP, W.

LAMBERT, H. J. L.
LANGMEAD, A. G.
LAUDER, J.
LEAR, C.
LEE, E. A.
LEWIS, A.
LIDDALL, P. R. J.
LITTLE, E.
LOEWY, J.
LORAM, W.
LOW, H. F.

MABSON, H.
MANNING, S. P. H. A.
MARCHANT, A.
MARTIN, A. R.
MARTIN, G.
MARTIN, H. C.
MARTIN, H. I.
MATTHEWS, C.
MATTHEWS, W.
MAWER, L.
MAY, C. R.
McMAHON, P.
MELHUISH, W. P. J.
MELLOR, A.
METCALFE, C. F. M.

MEWTON, E. R. L.
MICHELMORE, C. K. P.
MILNE, A. L.
MILTON, A. H.
MONK, F. I.
MOODY, H. V. C.
MORGAN, T. J.
MUDGE, D.
MUMBY, K. G. H.
MYOTT, P. M.

NANCEKIVELL, C. A.
NARRAMORE, P. W. F.
NEVILLE, F. V.
NICHOLLE, H. J.
NORTHCOTT, S.

OPIE, S. R.
OSBORNE, F. W.

PACKER, W. J. N.
PALMER, G. E.
PEDLER, S. J.
PERKINS, R. P.
PERKS, E. H.
PERRETT, R. G.
PERRY, L. L.
PETT, J. G. A.
PHILLIPS, A. J.
PHILLIPS, R. H.
PIKE, A. G.
POPE, M. H.
POTTER, H. J.
POWELL, J. W.
POWLESLAND, W. G.
POWNALL, F. W.
POWNET, J. E.
PURDY, J. I.
PUTT, W. J.
PYM, E. E. B.
PYNE, J. R.

RADFORD, F.
RADMORE, W. J.
RAISEY, E. C.
RAWLE, H. S.
RAYMONT, C. R.
REDFERN, B. W.
RICHARDS, J. R.
RIDER, H. E.
ROBINSON, A. W.
ROOK, H.
ROOPE, F. M.

RYDER, J.

SANDERS, L. C.
SANDERS, M. H.
SANSOM, A. T.
SATTERLEY, A. G.
SCOTT, P. W.
SCRIVINGS, H.
SHAMBROOK, E. H.
SHOBBROOK, L. A.
SMERDON, G. P.
SMITH, S. G.
SMITH, W.
SOLOWEICZYK, L. M.
SOUTHCOTT, W. E.
SPARKS, W. H.
SQUIRES, A. R.
STACEY, J. W.
STANLAKE, H. J.
STEER, A. H.
STEER, W. T.
STEVENS, W.
STEVENS, W. A.
STRACHAN, M.
SWEETLAND, H.

TANNER, R. J.
TAYLOR, G. W.
TAYLOR, H. T.
TERRY, G. B.
THORNE, T. H.
TOMBS, A.
TONKIN, R. T. H.
TOULSON, J.
TOWNSEND, J. F.
TUCKER, F. J.
TUCKER, S. H.
TURNER, N. J.
TYLER, D.

VANSTONE, R. G.

WALL, J. W.
WARD, G. H.
WARREN, E. S.
WEEKS, W. H.
WEIGHTMAN, A. W.
WELLS, P.
WHELAN, P.
WIDDICOMBE, H. P.
WILLIAMS, L. W. G.
WOOD, F. E.
WOOD, H. E.

"C" COMPANY

Major
WOOD, F., M.S.M.

Captains
CLARK, J.
HOPKINSON, E. C., M.C.

Lieutenants
AINSWORTH, A. L.
BURCH, H. J.
DEAKIN, H. J.
GRAINGER, H. W. S.
HADDOCK, E. H., M.C.
HERROD, G. G.
HICKS, R.
JARVIS, G. H.
KNIGHT, A. J.
MUGFORD, J. H., M.C.

UNDERHAY, R.
WHITE, F. G.

2nd Lieutenant
HEEKS, N.

C.S.M.
LAKE, R. S., M.M.

C.Q.M.S.
TOMLIN, H.

Sergeants
BAKER, W. G.
BARLEY, F. A.
BEER, S. J.
BEST, W. E.
CLEMENTS, H.

COLE, S.
CUDLIPP, H.
DONE, A. H. F.
DREW, F. J.
FAIRER, E. C.
GILLSON, W. M.
HEUGHAN, A.
LADDS, H. C.
LANGFORD, H.
LANGMEAD, L.
LEWIS, R. G.
LOCKE, W. J.
MORRIS, J.
MOTTS, E. N.
PASSMORE, S. A.
RICE, T. H.
ROBERTS, A. G.
SCOTT, W. T.

"C" COMPANY—continued

SEYMOUR, A. G. E.
SMITH, F. G.
WILLIAMS, H. E.

Corporals
ANDREWS, E. A.
ANSTEY, E. J.
ASH, A. E.
BAKER, R. J.
BISHOP, K. E.
BLOOMFIELD, E. E. H.
BOARD, C.
BOON, C. H.
BOWDEN, W. H.
BUTCHER, E. A.
CLARK, A. E.
CLIFF, A., O.B.E.
COATH, G. H.
COLE, F. G.
CORNEY, A. J.
COTTER, J.
CUNNINGHAM, J. G.
DOMINEY, R. W. L.
DRURY, W. G. H.
DULEY, A. E.
DYER, F. C.
EDWORTHY, W.
ESSERY, C. H.
GODFREY, H.
GREGORY, H. E.
HANNAFORD-HILL, A. J.
HINE, A. G.
HOLMES, E. S.
HORSHAM, P. G.
JACKSON, A.
JOHNS, G. H. C.
JOHNSON, L. T.
KEYWOOD, W. C.
LAWSON, W. C.
LEWIS, C.
LEWIS, L. G.
LITTLE, R. G.
LORD, V. D.
LUGG, T.
MOLLOY, C. E.
NEISH, H. C.
NORTHCOTT, J.
OWEN, H. I.
PAYNE, J. L.
PHILLIPS, N. S.
PHILLIPS, P. R.
RABBICH, F.
ROOST, H. C.
SHRUBSOLE, F.
SMITH, F. J.
STEPHENS, S. F.
VALE, J.
WATTS, E. S.
WESTERN, A.
WILLIAMS, F. J. H.
WINDSOR, A. E.

Lance Corporals
BATTERSHELL, J. V.
BELLAMY, R.
BRADFORD, W. E.
CARSON, L.
COE, P. J.
ELLIS, W. J. L.
ENDACOTT, F. E. J.
GARDINER, J. W.
GATIER, R. A. J.
HARRIS, J. D.
HOOPER, A. W.
HOTTEN, H. C.
ISAAC, J. H.
LANGLER, H. J.

LITTLEJOHNS, R. H.
MITCHELL, A. H.
NORMAN, L. J.
OLVER, P. E.
PARSONS, C.
POTHAM, A. T.
POTHAM, S. T.
ROWELL, F. G.
SPARROW, J. D. G.
STOCKER, T. W.
STONE, L. J.
TUCKER, F. S.
WRATZKE, F. E. E.

Privates
ADAMS, S. G.
ADAMS, W. E.
ALFORD, S. J.
ALLERY, L. J.

BADCOTT, E. G.
BAKER, O. F.
BALL, S. H.
BARKER, T. I.
BARON, S.
BEAGLEHOLE, S. F.
BEARDON, L. C.
BEER, F. W. J.
BELL, M. G.
BIBBINGS, F.
BICKLE, R. G.
BICKLE, T.
BINMORE, F. G.
BINMORE, R. F.
BLACKLEY, G.
BLAGDON, L. J.
BLAKE, E. C. C.
BLENK, A. E.
BOWHAY, G. A.
BRADY, V.
BRIDGMAN, W. P.
BRIMICOMBE, E. J.
BROWSE, R.
BUNKER, G. B.
BURNELL, A. E. G., M.S.M.

CARTER, S.
CAUNTER, A. W.
CHUBB, R.
CHUBB, R. H.
COCKER, E.
COCKS, K. A.
COLE, F. R.
COLE, R.
COLE, S. A.
COLE, S. T.
COLEBY, H.
COLLINGS, A. H.
COLLINGS, C.
COLLINGS, E.
COLLINGS, H.
COLLINGS, H. J.
COLLINGS, O. G.
COLLINGS, R. E.
COLLINS, E. H.
COSE, S. J.
COWLING, F.
COYSH, F. R.
CRAWFORD, C. G. W.
CREESE, H. S.
CREMONESI, I. R.
CRIMP, J.
CROOK, G. P.

DALTON, A.
DANIELS, E. G.
DAVIES, T.

DICKER, W. J.
DOBBIN, J. T.
DOBSON, T. E.
DREW, E. L.
DYER, L. E.

EKERS, H. E. C.
ELLIS, S. E.
EMMETT, R. J.
ENDACOTT, R. G. H.

FELDERMAN, C. C.
FERRIS, R.
FORD, J. H. J.
FORD, W. J.
FOSTER, F. J.
FOXWORTHY, C. O.
FRAIN, S. C.
FRENCH, J.
FUGE, F. J.
FUGE, P. P.
FULTON, E. A. C.
FURNEAUX, W. E.

GENTLE, A. W.
GILES, E. R.
GILL, W. A.
GOWLAND, J. G.

HAMMETT, A. J. C.
HAMMETT, G. E.
HARRIS, A. J.
HARRIS, A. R.
HATCHARD, A. F.
HAYES, A.
HEAD, R. T. P.
HELLEY, V. W. S.
HELLIER, S.
HICKEY, T. G.
HILL, P. J.
HINE, P.
HOLLIER, A.
HOLMES, A. E.
HOWARD, H.

JOHNSON, H.
JOYCE, J. B.

KELLY, C. P.
KEMBLE, A. J.
KENSHOLE, H. G.
KERSLAKE, L. E.
KIBBY, R. G.
KNAPMAN, E. J.
KNIGHT, H. P.

LANE, G.
LANG, J. H.
LANGDON, D.
LAVERS, R.
LEVERICK, A. E.
LIDGEY, W. J.
LITTLE, E. D.
LONG, F. C.
LOVERING, J. D.
LUSCOMBE, W.

MADDICK, S. J. E.
MADDICK, W. G.
MARKS, L. C.
MARLEY, P. L.
MARSHALL, W. S.
MATTHEWS, W. J.
MAY, W.
McCABE, M. J.
McKENDRICK, I.
McRAE, D. A.

"C" COMPANY—continued

MEDLAND, H.
MITCHELMORE, W. J.
MOGRIDGE, J.
MOREY, E.

NARRAMORE, L. V.
NEAL, C. W.
NEVILLE, C. W.
NEWPORT, E.
NICHOLLS, G. E.
NORMAN, F.

O'DONOGHUE, D.

PALFREY, F. G.
PASCOE, E.
PASCOE, P. J.
PAYNE, J. E.
PEARSE, A. W.
PEARSE, W. H.
PICKARD, R. G.
PIKE, H. C. T.
PIPER, W. J.
PITMAN, S. B.
PITMAN, S. W.
PLAICE, W. G.
PLOWMAN, A. J.

PONTIN, T. L.
PONTING, A. T.
POPPLESTONE, A. W. T.
POTTINGER, F.
PREISS, E. L. C., M.M.
PROWSE, S. C.
PULLEN, H. G.

RETTER, R. J. L.
RICHARDS, W.
RICHARDS, W. S.
ROBERTS, W.
ROPER, B.
ROUS, F. H.
ROWE, A. E.
RUMBELOW, W. H.
RUNDLE, W. R.

SALTER, N. J.
SAUNDERS, W. C.
SCOBLE, J. H.
SEWART, W. W.
SHEPPARD, E. H.
SHOVE, E. C.
SMALLRIDGE, S. M.
SMITH, V.

SQUIRES, E. J.
STOCKMAN, W.
STONE, C. S.
SWAINSON, W. F.
SYKES, C. W.

TAYLOR, A.
TAYLOR, M.
TEAGUE, H. C.
TOMS, D. W.
TOZER, R.
TRACE, W. H.
TREBY, P. J.
TUCKER, A. C.

UNDERHAY, M. F.

WALDRON, K. H.
WARREN, W. J.
WATSON, J.
WEBBER, A. G.
WEBBER, E. G.
WHEATCROFT, I. F.
WHITE, W.
WILLIAMS, F. C. J.
WOOLRIDGE, W. S.

"D" COMPANY

Major
PUGHE-MORGAN, R. B.

Captain
BIRCHAM, W. H. C.

Lieutenants
FARMER, E. G.
GORRELL, S. C.
GRIFFITHS, F.
NORVALL, A. F.
PEPPERELL, W. J.
PRICE, S. E. V.

2nd Lieutenants
MOUNTER, W. H.
TRIGGOL, E. T.
WILLIAMS, B. G.

C.S.M.
LIDSTONE, N. J.

C/Sergeant
ELPHICK, A. H

Sergeants
BROOM, W.
CATT, D. W.
COLEMAN, R.
DYER, A. P.
FINDEISON, K. D.
GARDNER, R. S. E.
GAVINS, C. A.
HARVEY, H. J.
HAYLOCK, G.
JONES, B. C.
KING, E. J.
MOCK, W. F.
SHERWIN, C.
SMARDON, W. R.
SQUIRES, J. H.
TAYLOR, A.
TEALE, F. J.
WIDDICOMBE, A. E. J.

WILLS, E. P.
WINSOR, W. C.
WOODMAN, H. H.

Corporals & Bombardiers
ANDERSON, F. N.
BEARMAN, W.
BRIDGE, H. J.
BROADLEY, A.
BUDD, W. H. T.
CHASE, B. M.
DART, E. H.
FOOT, W. R.
GAGG, P. A.
HEATH, R. H.
JORDAIN, E. V.
NICHOLLS, F.
PACK, H. J.
STAPLETON, W. E.
TREEBY, W. E.
TRUST, J. H.
UPHAM, H. H.
WORTH, M. G.
YOLLAND, W. L.

L/Corporals & L/Bombardiers
BASTOW, N. J.
BROKENSHIRE, S. A.
CARTER, R. M.
GLIDDON, E. A.
GREEN, C. A.
HARRIS, R. R.
HAYDEN, F. R.
HOPPER, R. H.
ISAAC, L. J.
ISAAC, P. G.
JOHNS, S. L.
KENNEDY, F. W.
LAKE, B.
LEY, F. D.
NEAL, D. W. G.
PETTS, J. E.
STABB, F. R.
STEER, S. E.

THATCHER, S. H.
TREEBY, J. F.
VALLANCE, W. A. de V.

Privates & Gunners
ANDREWS, R. E.
BASTIN, H. L.
BATTERSHALL, H. J.
BEARD, D. W.
BEHAR, D.
BERRY, H. H.
BLACKLER, W. H.
BODENA, W. J.
BOON, W. L.
BOWERS, F.
BOWLES, T. F.
BRIDGE, G. E.
BUCKLER, R. J.
BUDD, G. H.
BULEY, R. H.
BURWOOD, R. A. J.

CARR, G.
CHIPPS, E.
CLYBURN, W. J.
COLE, E. T.
COLLEY, G. E.
COLLIER, R. G.
COLLIER, T. G.
COTTRILL, G.
COUCH, W. J.
COWLING, E. J. H.
COYSH, T. W.
CRANG, R. R. H.
CRANG, S. J.
CRONIN, J. P.

DALLEY, H. F.
DALTON, W.
DART, P. J.
DAVIE, G. T.
DAVIE, W. C.
DIMOND, T. H.

"D" COMPANY—continued

DOWELL, J. W. B.
DRIVER, F. J.
DUNN, E. W.
DUNN, G. A.

EASTLEY, H. E.
ECCLES, R. B.
ECCLES, R. D.
EDGECOMBE, J. F.
EDWARDS, L.
ELLIOT, W. G.
ENDICOTT, W. F.
ESCOTT, A. H. C.
EVANS, H.
EVANS, S. H.

FARLEY, H. S.
FINCH, H. E.
FISHER, L. G.
FITZGERALD, W. J.
FOSTER, R.
FOX, E. F.

GAGG, R. G.
GARDNER, J. F.
GEDDES, W.
GERRY, T. J.
GILES, F. A.
GLANFIELD, G. J.
GREENHALGH, A. H.

HAMBLYN, E. C.
HAMLING, S. H.
HAMLYN, G.
HAMMETT, W. C.
HARRIS, R.
HARRIS, S. J.
HART, L. E.
HARVEY, W. S.
HAWKINS, R. J.
HAYMAN, D. J.
HOCKINGS, W. D.
HOCKINGS, S. T. G.
HODDER, E. H.
HOOPER, C. H.
HOOPER, J. T.
HUBBARD, W. G.

ISAAC, F. M.
ISAAC, F. C. J.

ISAAC, H. M.

JACKSON, G. T.
JACKSON, P. J. L.
JACKSON, R. L.
JAMES, H. P.
JONES, H.
JORDAIN, W. G.
JURY, A.
JURY, W. A.

KIMBLE, R.
KNAPMAN, W. G.
KNIGHT, R.
KNOWLES, W. F.

LANCASTER, F. D.
LANE, W.
LANGMAN, W.
LIDSTER, J. E. W.
LIDSTONE, A. C.
LONGTHORPE, S. E.
LORAM, E. G.
LUCKHAM, F.
LUCKHAM, W. C. J.
LUSCOMBE, F. J.
LUSCOMBE, W. J. A.

MAUNDER, F.
MELVILLE, K. J.
MEMERY, R. L.
MEREDITH, A. E.
MOORE, W. F.
MUGFORD, C.

NEWLAND, J. H.
NORTHEY, E. R.

PARISH, A. R.
PERCY, W.
PERRY, A.
PERRY, E. J.
PINE, R. L.
POCOCK, W. J.
PRESTON, W. F.
PRINCE, A. G.

RENDLE, F. G.
RENIER, E. W. A.

REYNOLDS, F. G.
REYNOLDS, G. S.
ROLLINGS, W. G.
RUNDLE, C. A.
RUNDLE, R. A.
RUNDLE, V. G.

SANDFORD, R. H.
SANDFORD, R. W. J.
SEAGRIM, W. J.
SEAWARD, R. J.
SHAW-LANG, O.
SHEARS, F. C.
SILMAN, W. T.
SIMPSON, F. R. B.
SKEDGEL, A.
SKEDGEL, F. H.
SKEDGELL, J. P.
SKINNER, W.
SMITH, N.
SMITH, S. J.
SNELL, W. T.
STABB, B.
STABB, W.

THOMPSON, A. S.
TOLCHER, R. H.
TRIGGOL, W. F.
TUCKER, L. F.
TULLY, W. C.
TURNER, F. C.

UPHAM, L. C.

WAGLAND, A. J.
WALLACE, R. G.
WARREN, J.
WEEKES, R. E.
WESTLAKE, R. D.
WHEWELL, J.
WHITE, J.
WILCOX, R. W.
WILLIAMS, A. L.
WILSON, S. G.
WOOD, A. H.
WOTTON, D. C.

YEOMAN, F.
YEOMAN, F. R.

"F" COMPANY

Major
BENTLEY, G. F. W. A.

Captain
HARRIS, R. J.

Lieutenants
BODDINGTON, T. C.
HILL, C. V.
NORTHCOTT, E.
OLIVER, G. H.
PYMAN, S.
SUTCLIFFE, A. K.
WILLIAMS, I. A.

2nd Lieutenants
BASTEN, L. R.
BREWSTER, F.
CROUCH, C. W.
DURNELL, H. W.
HARRIS, E. V.
STEWART, R. H.

C.S.M.
CALLOW, L. F.

C.Q.M.S.
OSBORNE, S.

Sergeants
AUSTIN, W. T.
BOSANKO, J. J. C.
BRYANT, H. E.
CLOAD, B.
CRANSTON, G. A. W.
DUCK, G. R.
FORCE, A. L.
FORD, R. G.
FRICKER, E. O.
GARD, H. V.
HAMILTON, P. H.
HANKINS, G.
HILL, W. H.
JENKINS, S.
KENTISPEARE, L. H.
LAMBLE, G.

LEGGETT, F.
MARTIN, L. W.
MATTHEWS, W. P.
MORE, J. C.
RAWLIN, W. E.
SAMBELLS, A. T.
SQUIRES, R. G.
STOCKER, C. B.
UNDERHILL, A. H.
VAIL, F. J.
WALKER, R.
WESTAWAY, F.
WILLMOT, L.
WISEMAN, T. H.
WOOD, W. T.

Corporals
BLOOMFIELD, C. W. S.
BRIDGEMAN, W. J.
CLARK, E. C.
COLLINGS, F. V.
DARBYSHIRE, T. L.
DAW, W. J.

"F" COMPANY—continued

EALES, S. C.
EGAN, E. M.
ELLIS, F. J.
EVANS, S.
HARDMAN, C.
HART, P. F.
HATHERLEY, L. C.
HAYWARD, H. G.
HERRA, D. J.
HUDSON, S. L.
JONES, R. E.
KERNICK, L. E.
MARSHALL, G.
MAUNDER, F. P.
MAUNDER, R. J.
PATTERSON, S. C.
POLLARD, H. C.
SHILLABEER, R. C. V.
SKENE, J. G.
SNELL, H.
VEALE, H. F.
WARN, J. T.
WHITE, S. H.
WILLCOCKS, S.
WILLS, F.

Lance Corporals
CLARK, H.
COLLINGS, T. R.
COPLEY, W. H.
CREMONESI, A.
GAY, W. C.
GOODCHILD, C. R.
GRAHAM, J. F.
HARVEY, J. H. L.
MORTIMORE, H.
NEIGHBOUR, E. T.
PORT, W. E.
REED, H. R.
RICKARD, V. R.
ROBINSON, J. C.
SIMPSON, R. L.
STEART, A. B.
SYMS, G. H.
WEBBER, H. P.
WHITE, F. C.
WILKS, S. S.

Privates
ARCHER, T. G.

BARBER, H. J.
BASTONE, A. E.
BATCHELOR, E.
BAWDEN, W.
BELL, A. J.
BILLINGS, J. R.
BLACKBURNE, C. G. C.
BOARD, F. J.
BOLAS, C. F.
BOND, J. E.
BOURNE, B. J.
BRIGGS, T. H.
BRIMELOW, W. H.
BROOKING, A. F.
BROOKING, L. H.
BROWN, A. G.
BROWN, F. J.
BUCKINGHAM, J. W.
BUSH, G. B.

CAFFIN, J. E.
CARTER, F.
CATCHPOLE, H. R.
CATTELL, S. N.
CAVANNA, R. E.
CAWDLE, H. W.

CHATEL, E. J.
CLARK, G. A.
COFFIN, F. H.
COKER, F. R.
COLE, F. T. F.
COLLACOTT, A. R. I.
COOPER, J. R.
COCPER, W. F. A. D.
COWLING, R. G.
CRISP, R. A.
CURLE, S. L.

DAMARELL, J. C.
DAVIES, S. B.
DELANY, C. J.
DENHAM, H. J.
DOWELL, F. A.
DOWLING, H. T.

EVANS, G. J. W.
EVANS, J.

FISHER, F.
FOLEY, W. A.
FOSTER, C. M.
FOSTER, H.
FRENCH, C. H.
FRENCH, F. B.
FRENCH, H. J.
FRIEND, W.

GABLER, H. M.
GAMBRELL, H. J.
GENTRY, G. G.
GEOGHEGAN, D.
GERMAN, P.
GIBBINGS, F. C.
GILBERT, A. A.
GOFF, W. W.
GOSS, L. F.
GOSS, L. T.
GOVER, W. E.
GREAVES, G. L.
GREENWELL, R.
GRIFFIN, F. H.
GRIFFITHS, L.

HALEY, A. R.
HALLETT, R. G.
HANN, W. G.
HANNAFORD-HILL, A. J.
HARRIS, W. R.
HART, C. J.
HATHERLEY, F. E.
HAYNES, H. H.
HEAD, G. H.
HEAD, H. E.
HEALE, W.
HEATH, C. J.
HEDGES, A. J.
HENNION, P. G. W.
HILL, G. E. H.
HILL, R. P.
HOCKING, O. F.
HOLLAND, A. E.
HOWE, P. J.
HOWELL, G. H.
HUMPHRIS, G.
HYAMS, D.

ISAACS, V. W.

JEWELL, J.
JEWELL, W. J.
JOHNSON, F. J.
JONES, J. R.

JONES, T. E.

KEAST, M. B.
KEMBLE, L. S.
KEMP, T.
KEY, J. R.
KITT, A. W.
KITT, G. G.
KLIEFF, E.
KNAPMAN, D. F.

LAFFORD, W. T.
LANGDON, H.
LAWLESS, A. G.
LEEDS, G. G. M.
LEWORTHY, W. G.
LIGHT, J. H.
LOW, A. J.

MADGE, F. E.
MAKER, D. L.
MANLEY, A. D.
MANLEY, V. G.
MARTIN, F. C.
MARTIN, G. W.
MARTIN, W. J.
MATTHEWS, R. E.
MEAD, J. R.
MICHEL, L. M.
MICHELL, R. E.
MILFORD, B. P.
MILLER, S. H.
MITCHELMORE, B. G.
MITFORD-BARBERTON, G. de B.
MORGAN, J. F.
MORTIMORE, L. M.
MORTIMORE, M.
MORTIMORE, S. J.
MUDGE, C. W. E.
MUGFORD, F. J.
MURPHY, T. J.

O'BRIEN, P.
OPIE, R. G.

PARKER, A. V.
PARKER, R.
PARNELL, P. J.
PAYNE, W. R.
PEARSON, D. H.
PENGILLY, W.
PENNY, W. C.
PERRAM, T. P.
PERRYMAN, T. C. A.
PETERS, E. C. G.
PETERSEN, M. K.
PIKE, H. C.
PIGGOTT, S.
PIPER, S. J. C.
PODRO, J.
PRICE, A. W.
PROUT, G. H.
PROUT, H. V.
PROWSE, J. H.
PROWSE, W.

READ, B. E.
ROSEVEARE, O.
RUNDLE, L. A.
RYCROFT, G.

SAUNDERS, F. S.
SAVAGE, V. M.
SELWAY, H.
SEYMOUR, T. S.
SHAPLEY, J. J.

"F" COMPANY—continued

SHILVOCK, A.
SHUTE, F. J.
SNELL, L. G.
SOPP, G. E.
STEVENS, W. H.
STOCKMAN, A.
STRIKE, R. M.
SWINNERTON, B. R.

TEAGUE, H. C.
THOMPSON, C. F.
THOMPSON, J. L.
TOZER, J. A.
TREBILCOCK, F.

TUCKETT, S.

UNDERHAY, F. J.
UTLEY, J.

VINCENT, W. H.
VOSPER, L. G.

WATSON, C. N.
WEBBER, F. J.
WEBBER, W. H.
WHEEN, C. H.
WHITAKER, W. J.
WHITE, T. S.
WHITWORTH, S. G.

WILKINS, C. G.
WILLIAMS, E. J.
WILLIAMS, Y. T. M.
WILLIAMSON, J.
WILLICOTT, P.
WILLIS, G.
WILLIS, G. A.
WILLS, G.
WILSON, A. E.
WILSON, H. A.
WOOD, H.
WOODBRIDGE, L. A.
WORTH, A. G.

YEO, A. G.

"H" COMPANY

Lt.-Colonel
SLOGGETT, A. J. H., D.S.O.

Majors
BALL, W. F., T.D.
WARWICK, F. P., D.S.O.
WOOSLEY, E. H., C.B.E.

Captains
BAYLEY, L.C.C.
GARRETT, Sir J. H., K.C.I.E.,

C.S.I.
GRANT, H.
READ, P. T., M.B.E., M.M.
TAYLOR, R. C., M.B.E., M.M.

Lieutenants
ADE, J. E. D.
BEHAR, M. E.
DENTON, J. W., G.M.
GAY, F. C.
HALLION, W. F.
KERNICK, W. H. L.
OLIVER, L. W.
OLLERENSHAW, F.
PETERS, H. W.
PITMAN, J. G.
RICH, J. B.
SAMSON, W. H.
SHERLOCK, G.
STRIKE, A. W.

2nd Lieutenants
CLIFFORD, H.
HARDING, W. H.
VANDERHOOF, W. B.

R.Q.M.S.
FLETCHER, R. A.

C.S.M.
SCUDAMORE, J. A.

S/Sergeant
HUTCHINGS, H. E.

A. S/Sergeant
WHEATLEY, A.

Sergeants
ASHOON, E. A. J.
CLIFF, F. W.
COWLING, F. B.
FRASER, D.

GELDARD, H.
HIDER, G. J.
HOLLOWAY, W. A.
LANE, W. T.
McDONALD, H. G.
NICKELS, J.
RENDELL, F. T.
RICHARDSON, F. C., G.M.
RICHARDSON, P.
TOZER, J. R.
TUCKER, L.
WILKINSON, P.
WILLIAMS, F. C. P.

A/Sergeants
BOWE, C. T.
WEINER, P. L. I.

L/Sergeant
WALKEY, P. J.

Corporals & Bombardiers
BELL, F.
BLACKLER, G. E.
BORER, S.
BROWN, A. C.
CHAPPLE, J. H.
CLAPHAM, G. N.
COOPER, S. A.
DUGGLEBY, H. D.
GILBERT, A. G.
HARRIS, G. E.
HEBBES, P.
HEMINGWAY, G. A.
HEXTER, W. T.
HURRELL, H. F.
JEFFERY, J.
JONES, L.
KELLOW, G. F.
LALES-ALLEN, J. G. N.
NEWMAN, P. P.
PADBURY, J.
PALK, R. W. J.
PORTER, D. W. A.
POULTON, J. A.
PRICE, A. E.
TOMS, A.
WORSFOLD, W. F.

L/Corporals & L/Bombardiers
BAILEY, A. F.
BELL, R.
BULLEID, L. T.
COCK, W. D.
COLE, L.

GATTING, H. R.
GIBBINGS, T. H.
GOLDING, G. F.
GRILLS, H. V.
HARRIS, W. J.
HILL, C. H.
HOOPER, F. C.
JEFFERY, G. A.
JENNINGS, W.
LLOYD, J.
PEMBERTON, K. G.
ROBINSON, G. E.
SPENCER, T. W.
TRAFFORD, N.
WEEKS, H. D.
WITHERS, C. A.

Privates & Gunners
ALFORD, H.
ALFORD, W. S.
ALLEN, C. P.
ALWOOD, F. C.
ANNEAR, F. T. C.
ARNOLD, H.

BAILEY, F. M.
BANNISTER, G. C.
BARNARD, P. J.
BARTLETT, S. E.
BEER, V. C.
BENNETT, A. H.
BENNETT, R. S. N.
BENNETT, W. L.
BINDING, W.
BIRD, W. R.
BLOWER, L. W. R.
BODDY, W. J.
BOND, W. F.
BRAILEY, E. G. C.
BROOKS, B.
BOYCE, W. J.
BROWN, A. C.
BUCKMASTER, H. W.

CAMILLERI, S.
CAMPBELL, R.
CANN, W. J.
CATER, F. J.
CHAPPLE, A. W.
CLARK, R. J.
CLEMENTS, E.
COCKS, H. A.
COHEN, B. W.
COLE, A. C. J.
COLE, H. F.

"H" COMPANY—continued

COLE, R. S.
COLEMAN, F. C.
COLES, J. H.
COLLINGS, G. H.
COLLINGS, W. J.
CORBY, J. E.
COVE, E.
COX, T. J.
CRIDGE, D. H.
CUSS, C. G.
CUSS, R. A.

DALL, J. A.
DAVIES, D. C.
DAVIES, P.
DAVIS, L. J.
DAWE, R. R.
DIXON, G. P.
DIXON, L. F.
DOWRICK, P.
DREW, S. J.
DYSON, W. R.

EAST, A. E.
EASTON, W. J.
EDWARDS, F. D. C.
ELLIS, F. C.
ESCOTT, W. E.
EVERARD, E.

FARLEIGH, W. R.
FARLEY, F. E.
FINCH, R. P.
FORWARD, J.
FOSTON, R. H.
FRANKS, W. J.
FREDMAN, L. B.

GERRY, P.
GILBERT, T.
GILPIN, G. E.
GOODING, J. H.
GOULD, F. E.
GOULD, V. H.
GRAHAM, H.
GREEN, F. C.
GREEN, F. E.
GREEN, F. S.
GREEN, G. S.
GRILLS, L. P.

HACON, R. C.
HAMMETT, F. J.
HARPER, B.
HARVEY, P. C.
HARVEY, W. H.
HASLETT, J.
HAWKINS, J. D. C.
HEATHERSHAW, C
HIGBEE, A. R.
HIGGINS, W. H.
HISCOX, P. H.
HOLMAN, C. J. E.
HOLMES, E. C.
HOLWILL, F. J.
HOOPER, A. G.
HOOPPELL, B. H.
HORSFALL, J. T.
HUNT, J. H.
HUNTER, S.

INGRAM, L.
IRWIN, C. R.

JOHNS, E. E.
JOHNSTON, O. G.

KENNEFORD, S. T.
KINBER, L. F. C.

LAMBLE, J. W. E.
LANDER, F. J.
LANE, J. W.
LANE, S. G.
LAW, L. J.
LAWRENCE, R. W.
LEAMAN, F. E.
LEAMAN, L. A. J.
LEWIS, D. H.
LEWIS, G. H.
LEWIS, V.
LITTLE, H.
LOCKE, L. J.
LOCKE, N.
LYLE, A. E.

MADDOCK, P. J.
MARTIN, G. A. E.
MARTIN, P. D.
MASLIN, E. L.
MATHER, W. A. V.
MAUNDER, D. J.
MAUNDER, N. B.
MAUNDER, R. S. G.
MEAD, G.
MILFORD, E. G.
MILLSOM, L.
MOATES, W. G.
MOIST, A.
MOREY, F.
MORRIS, R. J.
MOSEDALE, F. J.
MOXHAY, H.
MUGFORD, E. J.
MYHILL, G.

NEWBAND, C. J.
NEWBERRY, D. G.
NEWNHAM, W. R.
NICHOLLS, W.
NICHOLLS, P. H.
NORTHEY, F. P.
NORTHWAY, W. J. G.
NUTTALL, W.

PEDLER, W.
PERRAM, P.
PHILLIPS, R.
PIERCE, A.
PILLAGE, J. R.
PORCELLI, A.
PORT, A. J.
POWELL, E. W.
POWELL, F.
POWLING, F. H.
PROWSE, J. H.
PUDDICOMBE, F. S.
PULLEN, R. B.
PURFIELD, H. H.
PYNE, F. J.
PYNE, P. T.

REDDING, H. G. P.
RENDELL, R. L.
RENDLE, C. H.
RENDLE, G. L.
RESSTONE, R. L.
RICE, A.
RICE, C. D.
RICE, N. E.

RICHARDS, A. W.
RICHARDS, F. T.
RIDSDALE, J. A.
ROBERTS, A. F.
ROBERTS, R. W.
ROGERS, J.

SAUNDERS, F. E.
SAUNDERS, T. E.
SEWART, P. O.
SHEPHERD, H. J.
SHEARS, H.
SIBLEY, E. W.
SMITH, J. W.
SOPER, F. H.
SOPER, F. T.
SOUTHWOOD, H.
SPILLER, W. J.
STEPHENS, G. L.
STEVENS, A.
STEVENS, R. J.
STONE, E.
STRICKLAND, H. J.
SWEENEY, B.
SYMONS, B. E.

TANCOCK, R. R. J.
TARRANT, J. G.
THEODORE-JONES, E.
THORNE, R.
TILLEY, C. A.
TIPPLES, A.
TOLLY, C. F. A.
TOUSSAINT, C. A.
TOWELL, H.
TOZER, H.
TOZER, H. V.
TROTT, E. C.
TRUSCOTT, B. G. E.
TRUST, W. J.
TURNER, S.

VANSTONE, J. F.
VEYSEY, F. G.
VICKERY, C. E.
VINTON, R.

WAKEHAM, B.
WALDRON, R. G.
WEBBER, A. H.
WEBBER, M. E.
WEDDEN, H.
WEEKS, L. H.
WEISS, C.
WELLS, W. T.
WENALEY, A. G.
WESTAWAY, A. A. C.
WESTERN, L. J.
WHITE, C. A.
WILKINS, E. C. S
WILLIAMS, C. L.
WILLIAMS, E.
WILLIAMS, M. E.
WILLIS, W. T. H.
WINDEATTE, H. G.
WINSOR, F. J.
WINSOR, F. M.
WOODWARD, R. A.
WOOLER, J.
WORDEN, S.
WYATT, E. F.

YEO, M. H.
YOUNG, C. H

The Last Word...

That most jealously preserved of editorial prerogatives—the right to the last word—is now used to repair an omission. No mention has been made of the womenfolk, whose patience, tolerance and co-operation were essential, yet they, too, made sacrifices and their support is gratefully acknowledged. We hope this little book will confirm their husbands' version of Home Guard service ; that they will forgive the spoiled Sunday dinners, the late suppers and the muddy boots. They were long suffering but served us well. We thank them.

www.ingramcontent.com/pod-product-compliance
Lightning Source LLC
Chambersburg PA
CBHW070546090426
42735CB00013B/3088